Reinholder to Rainmaker

Reinholder to Rainmaker, First Edition, copyright 2013 by Karen Delchamps. All rights reserved. No part of this publication may be reproduced, stored in a retrieval system, or transmitted in any form or by any means; electronic, mechanical, photocopying, or recorded without written permission from Karen Delchamps Books.

REINHOLDER TO
RAINMAKER

WE ALL HAVE THE POWER TO MAKE
IT RAIN

KAREN DELCHAMPS

Karen Delchamps Books

St. Louis Missouri

I thank My Father; He blesses me in unimaginable ways.

An immeasurable ration of gratitude to Heather and Jim Moresi; two people who demonstrated the quiet and selfless acts of kindness that Jesus taught while here on earth. You inspire me to be a better person. Words can't describe how grateful I am to you both.

This book is dedicated to them, Adam Wolf, Kaitie Eisenbath, Travis Kliethermes, Jeff Leckrone, Tim Leckrone, Colleen McKeon, Karin Orf and all of the great Samaritans that helped in my time of need. I am in awe of you.

I thank my parents, Paul and Joy Delchamps, who would go to the ends of the earth for their family. It is wonderful to be loved and supported to that magnitude.

And of course to my children; who fulfill my life daily with amazing bliss.

Foreword 11

Preface 15

Chapter 1} A New Thought 1

Diagram to the Dream 22

Chapter 2} Discern For Yourself 26

The Peace Compass 32

Chapter 3} Love God First 36

Faith 36

Prayer 40

Praise 48

Follow His Commandments 50

Believe 53

Repentance 57

Seek 59

Chapter 4} Misinterpretations of Our Forefathers 62

Evolution Verses Creation 62

Consumption of Alcohol 65

Drug Use 66

Surgery, Artificial Insemination, and Medicine 66

Birth Control 69

Divorce 69

Homosexuality 71

Promiscuity, Pre-marital Sex, Masturbation, and Unconventional Sex 75

Chapter 5} Loving EVERYONE 78

As We Love Ourselves 79

Without Judgment 83

Avoid Gossip and Wrong Doing 85

Separation of Church and Church 88

Chapter 6} Loving You for You 98

Chapter 7} Giving Alms & Doing Works 108

Chapter 8} The Missing Facet of the Reinholder 115

Chapter 9} The Final Test of The Reinholder 120

Chapter 10} The Facets of the Rainmaker 124

Peace 124

Poise 125

Power 129

Bringing word to power… 133

Abundance and Prosperity 136

Chapter 11} The Rainmaker 142

Foreword

We moved to The Midwest from Phoenix a few years ago. Unlike our former city of residence, St. Louis is notorious for its vast array of weather conditions from sizzling hot summers, fairly frigid winters, and boisterous thunderstorms to the unpredictability of the autumn season's temperatures. Yet even on the coolest of fall nights, it is not uncommon in our fairly small corner of suburbia for this neighbor or that to drag the fire pit dead center of the driveway and set a wood pile to blaze. It's the beacon that signals the message to our quaint little neighborhood "let's get together, have a beer, and visit". It was at one of these impromptu autumn get togethers that my wife and I got to know our new neighbor (she'd just moved in) for the first time.

She informed me that she was a writer, and when I questioned as to what, I was told I probably wouldn't be interested. I pressed and she told me she wrote about the scriptures; kind of a new age translation of it. I remember thinking "probably just a bible beater writing about the same old things, but it was the "new age translation" part that I must admit intrigued me a little.

As the middle son of an extremely religious family, the Bible was always pushed on me and I was repeatedly told what I could NOT do according to scripture. It was always "you can't do this, or you shouldn't do this or you will look bad in the eyes of God". I started believing that God was this tyrant of a deity that if we didn't do what He said He would strike us down. Needless to say, scripture and religion left a bad taste in my mouth.

As a young adult, I completely abandoned religion as well as the Bible. I knew what was right and wrong, and I believed that if I did what was right, I would remain in good standings in the eyes of God.

When I first read **Reinholder to Rainmaker**, it was like a breath of fresh air! Finally someone had a common sense view on scripture that I could get on board with. Karen Delchamps writes that God wants us to be happy, love one another, and live life to its fullest. She explains the scriptures are not what we shouldn't do, more just guidelines on how to live our life following the rules that He asked us to follow.

Her 20th century views make it easy to understand what the scriptures mean, and she brings it into light for a new generation. Karen bears her sole in her writings, and holds nothing back. From excerpts out of her personal journal and her first hand life experiences, she takes the reader through her triumphs as well as hardships. Within and in the midst of her struggles, Karen reveals her unwavering faith in

God. Adamantly clear to me, this person not only writes about faith but believes and lives by it every day.

As with any book, you may not agree with all of what she has to say, but you can't argue her dedication, love of her work, and desire to spread a new message of faith.

As an inspirational writer, Karen does not disappoint. Whether you are looking to find faith in God, or just rediscovering your own, you will find the starting point here. I have no doubt that this book has the ability to change your life profoundly as well as your views on God and scripture as it did mine.

Never in a million years would I have thought to tell you that I read an inspirational book and enjoyed it, much less read it multiple times, yet I am telling you just that!

I believe that for far too long the Bible has been thought of as something that our grandparents and parents read, and it was not really meant for a new generation. After reading **Reinholder to Rainmaker**, I firmly believe that to be incorrect. With her intensely fresh outlook, I believe the Bible can draw not only this younger generation, but many generations to come.

It is my sincere hope that you will find this book as compelling and insightful as I have.

-James Frank

Preface

For the first time since the origins of Christianity, experience The Bible the way God intended; as a seeker with an open mind and nonjudgmental heart. Now is the time to discard everything you were taught through generations of personal agendas, begin like an innocent and ignorant child and unfold the beautiful mysteries that God made just for you.

You have a divine destiny and it is huge! Every person in your life, every past experience you've had, every place that you have stepped and every thought that you've encompassed has lead you to today. There is a quintessential moment in your life when you must decide if you are to unlock that huge destiny, or simply continue to live in the status quo.

God has never lied. He tells us that we are promised HUGE prosperity, an ABUNDANCE of happiness, a WEALTH of healthiness, and a life filled with OVERALL victory. In scripture, He plainly states what we must do to receive our INCREDIBLE destiny.

Unfortunately, generations of well-intentioned followers have clouded and even covered that destiny. Misinformation has diverted our paths. Behaviors that we were taught were wrong enable us to judge our neighbors and fellow man, behaviors we were taught were pleasing to God, in many instances God never wanted of us.

Now is the time to forget what you were taught by others and begin the journey to your great destiny; the one that was ordained ONLY for you. Open your mind and heart and learn the secret to having every single miracle that God wants just for you. Set aside the notion that you have to become a religious freak, a bible thumper or a Christian nut. This is a spiritual journey that doesn't require conversation regarding Jesus at the water cooler. This is personal and comfortable.

Don't wait another day. Today is the day that life becomes simple with a quiet beauty and stillness that comes only from having absolutely everything that was intended just for you.

Chapter 1} A New Thought

Prepare to be disturbed. Be ready for big questions with different answers.

"Those who seek should not stop seeking until they find. When they find, they will be disturbed. When they are disturbed, they will marvel, and will rule over all."

-Jesus from the Gospel of Thomas

Whether we were raised as Christians and believe Jesus is The Son of God or believe, as the Muslim or Jewish religions, that Jesus was a great prophet, His teachings while on Earth were profound. His lessons held the essence for living a life in faith. There is no denying the brilliance of His parables or the clarity and wisdom of His observations.

"Those who seek should not stop seeking until they find." The first sentence is magnificent. Jesus knew that in our modern day world, it would be impossible to find the answers to the secrets of The Kingdom without seeking. He understood that most of us would never wander beyond the confines of a bible study group or our local church for answers.

There is a comfort in that, after all. If we listen to our pastor or priest's discernment of The Bible, we are comfortable in the coziness of a good man doing the work for us. But there is a danger far greater than we realize; relying on someone else to discern the truth and relay to us is not seeking but rather cheating. The result will be much the same as cheating our way through Medical School; we may become a doctor in name but will never have real success or real reward until we back up, regroup, and learn for ourselves.

Please don't misunderstand; there are many great pastors that are on the right path and teach correct scripture. But because it is their primary job to spread God's word, there will be certain areas he or she will avoid for the greater good of laying a foundation for faith within his congregation. Many pastors, priests, and ministers are well aware of the facts I will discuss in this book. It is impossible for them to discern scripture without a high level of awareness and pragmatic wisdom. But they will deliberately not divulge; not because of deception or ill-intent, but simply because it is their job to point us in the direction to a relationship with God. It is also their job to make their church flourish, pay the bills, build attendance, and create tithers. They have your best interest at heart as they gently lead you to seek and find what they cannot utter; what they themselves know.

That is why it is essential to our faith that we discern for ourselves what God asks of us. If like most, you will be upset with the findings; hence the second sentence, "when they find, they will be disturbed". You will be upset because the truth you thought you knew was only a fraction of the data needed; and with new knowledge holds new responsibility. You will be disturbed because your life long belief system instilled by parents, church, and society contained false information. This is indeed disturbing and upsetting.

But as the dust settles and the truth begins to resonate peace, like a hot pink tulip sprung into full bloom; we begin to feel complete. Yes, we are amazed… to the point of bliss and even euphoria. We will have a new sense of self that cannot be obtained by any other action than that of seeking.

This book is unlike any you've read thus far. It contains an unconventional message and ideas no one has ever emitted. But your job as a seeker is to read it, and decide for yourself based on your knowledge of God and scripture, if the ideas and logic is fact or fiction. It is your responsibility as His creation and follower to seek the truth and live by the rules He mandated; not that of man. This truth will set you free.

Aw, but the third sentence through Thomas of Jesus is the most exciting part of all! Jesus says "they will marvel and rule over all". They, the seekers, the ones that find what God wants from them, will rule over all. That is me, that is you, that is anyone that takes the time to learn the truth, makes the changes in his life, and deletes the practices that man said we should follow in the name of God. **We are the seekers who will rule over all!**

Inspirational and self-help books are written for two reasons; to guide others down the road to success and to sell books. Many indicate that the power of positive thinking, having a winning attitude, organizational skills and goal setting are the keys to success. Those are great traits to have but will not ensure success, wealth, and happiness. The fact is, God gives us specific clarification in what we are to do, but in this year of 2013, the message has been muffled, stifled, misinterpreted, misrepresented, misspoken, miscommunicated, and miswritten to the point of utter confusion.

One of my favorite authors, Emmet Fox (New Thought Spiritual Leader, 1886-1951), defines a form of prayer called scientific prayer. Scientific prayer is a step by step ritual that involves thanking God for all that is good in life, meditating on all of the great aspects of God, bringing the desires of your heart before Him in verbal communication and quiet meditation.

I tried it once; it didn't work. I was completely disappointed. The thing that I gave Him in prayer, I was desperate for, and because I had been reading The Bible daily, praying, and reading everything Fox and others had written regarding faith, it should have worked. Well, I cannot discredit such an honorable and knowledgeable author such as Fox, because the fault lied within me.

There is only one way to receive all of the desires of your heart and once you find that way; God will take all of your wishes, wants, and requirements and multiply them so many times you will not be able to comprehend the quantity to derive the precise equation He used.

God has an amazing life waiting for each and every one of His children. Had I studied Fox's teachings in great depth, my prayers would have worked. I missed the most important premise of his teachings; that only through a complete relationship with God and following His rules will our prayers be answered.

Additionally, in modern day until we can cast aside the misinformation of generations of misinterpretations of scripture, we will never take delivery of all He has to offer.

It is up to us to stop feeling guilty about our actions that God never cared about in the first place and start implementing actions that God wanted from us since the beginning of time.

This book is not for the traditional bible thumper, but for those that continue to try to do all the right things, are certain they are on the right path, only to find unanswered prayers and dreams unfulfilled. God is not answering your prayers for the same reason He didn't answer mine. I did the work, I did everything I was told; it just wasn't the assignment **God** gave me. It was an assignment from man; go to church, pray, tithe, do works and be a good person. Again, all great things to do and God likes them all, but God asks of us three specific requests; love Him, ourselves, and others.

Now if like me, you may think to yourself if that is all I need to do, then I am ready to receive. I do all of those things. But it is complicated. That is why Jesus says that we see a sliver of wood in someone else's eye but we cannot see a timber in our own. As easy as it is to believe that we can look within ourselves objectively, as Jesus points out, it's a difficult self-evaluation. Looking closely in the mirror for our own faults requires an objectivity most of us don't possess. **That is often why we are given tests, not as punishment but as a lesson in self-awareness.**

I can tell you just when I thought I had all the answers there was more to learn and always will be. But I am living the best and happiest life I have ever experienced.

Today starts now. Today is the day to discern TRUTH for ourselves, implement His plan, and receive The Promise.

At this writing, I would like to reveal to you what was revealed to me. It was just one book by Fox that set the precedence of a new life for me in seeking. If you have purchased this book it is no accident. There is a seed deep within us that thirsts for the truth. Also within that seed is a yearning for an extraordinary life. Both the truth and an extraordinary life can **only** be obtained through The Divine. We did not choose to feel this way; we were chosen. We ache for the dream.

John 15:16

"Ye have not chosen Me, but I have chosen you."

We often see on social media good-hearted people claiming "once you choose Jesus as your Lord and Savior, you will receive". If Jesus simply wanted our vote, He would have said so. Pay close attention to the requirement; Luke 6 is a great example. Jesus says those that believe in me AND live as I say…

Luke 6:48

He is like a man which built an house, and digged deep, and laid the foundation on a rock; and when the flood arose, the stream beat vehemently upon that house, and could not shake it: for it was founded upon a rock.

Jesus told us how to win. Whether you're in your twenties or in your seventies, your time to receive has come. Understand that all of the failed endeavors prior to now have a common denominator; the absence of divine power and ultimate wisdom.

Most of us believe through the teachings of our past that in order to live in faith our life must be ordinary and sacrifices must be made. I've heard people say "I'll be religious someday but right now I want to have fun".

We've been duped into believing that if we consume alcoholic beverages, dance, enjoy sex, or just enjoy life that we can't live in faith. It's completely opposite. God wants nothing less for us than to derive pleasure from life. It is an insult to God to even insinuate his disapproval of fun.

Don't be afraid to pleasure in life and reap all the rewards He has in store for you. Brace yourself for the incredible journey to great health, happiness and ultimate prosperity through faith in God.

When we begin to seek, God is as excited as we are. Conversely, if we stop seeking, He is hugely disappointed. That is why Jesus says once we seek, we should not stop. Once we are holding the reins of the seeker; we become a reinholder.

Luke 9:61-62

And another said "Lord, I will follow thee, but first let me go bid them farewell, which are at home at my house." And Jesus said unto him, "No man, having put his hand to the plough, and looking back is fit for the kingdom of God".

This is a hugely powerful parable given by Jesus. He is not saying that in order to seek, we must sacrifice our family and friends. It has nothing whatsoever to do with sacrifice as clearly defined in His next sentence. Jesus says once we BEGIN to seek, if there is a reason that is important enough to place our seeking on hold, we have officially placed a person, action, job, or entity before God. He concludes with the obvious…we are not fit for the kingdom. We have broken the first commandment. While He will forgive the sin, we have omitted ourselves from all that He has to offer. That is what we learn in the story of Job; that no event should alter our faithfulness to God.

Before the industrial revolution when man ploughed a field with a horse, it was a commitment of the entire day. It was not something started and stopped every hour or so because of the nature of the job. A man must first prepare the horse with nourishment and hydration. He then attached the harness and plough. The last act before the horse began to pull was the man firmly grasping and holding the reins. Once the man felt he had everything in order and the reins were comfortable in his hands, the long day would begin. He would have confidence that he had handled all of the smaller jobs and tended to his family so as not to have to drop the reins; he was committed to finishing the job.

The first word in the title is Reinholder because it represents those who are committed to seeking until they find. From the moment they pick up the reins, they never put them down until they have the power to make it rain. God promises us we will have the ability through prayer; our spoken word to fulfill every dream.

Literally, there are people in this world that can make it rain. They can move mountains, maintain a happy marriage, make more money than they know what to do with, and have the health and vitality of a twenty year old no matter how much they age. They are not a small minority but a rising statistic. You may know one, but it is your time to be one.

Because pain has a tendency to lead us to faith, recent events and the presence of turmoil have created a shift in numbers. Just like the economy and gravity, what goes up must come down. There was a time when the world seemed faithless and bleak, families were not in church and God was taken from the public eye.

But mankind is not unwise. We have the ability to sift through the rubble in the midst of turmoil and find the answer. There is only one constant since the beginning of time that over ninety percent of the world agree upon and that is the existence and power of One True God.

In the last chapter, entitled The Rainmakers, read of the joy, glory, prosperity, and bliss in store for all of us that make the commitment to pick up the reins. As you read it, let your heart fill with anticipation as you become ready to receive and let the peace that you feel give you a calm poise knowing of the power you will soon hold.

It isn't difficult and we don't have to be hyper intelligent or commit a large portion of the day to it. In fact, it doesn't require any additional time, it requires a change of mindset and a thirst for truth.

The following chapters are dedicated to a new plan; an absolutely definitive list of what is required and mandatory for the change of a lifetime; the recipe for the supernatural ultimate. I'm not an expert and I don't consider myself smarter or more intellectually apt to discern scripture more than the next person; anyone who takes the time to seek can surely find.

In my twenties, I read a celestial prophecy book that hugely inspired me but nothing changed. In my thirties, I read a book about "the secret" that left me ultimately unchanged as well. After reading Fox's teachings of the method of scientific prayer and exasperating with failure, I became dedicated to the experimentation myself.

It was ONLY when I cast out all that I had learned; became like a child and a blank page; that the true answers began to surface. I went to scripture, discovered the missing link, and a new me emerged. Sure I had learned many valuable facets through my readings, but I had learned an equal amount of false information and behaviors that quite literally kept me from receiving.

Too many people in this world are following the wrong rules; I was. This is the day it all changes. Start right now making the easy changes and watch your life transform before your eyes. There is no reason in the world that we cannot travel the world, party like a rock star, own a beautiful home, have a fun-filled, abundantly blessed and happy life. Our Father wants each and every child of His to excel and prosper. But it starts with an entirely different system.

When I read that first book in my twenties, I will never forget the day my younger brother David, suggested I purchase and read it. I went to the book store excited with anticipation of the idea of a happily and joyfully fulfilled new life. David had just finished it and had become vegetarian as a result of the inspiration the book had exuded. He relayed how a friend and many of his co-workers had read the book and was equally inspired. As I began my experience with this book, I remember thinking if David and I learned and could implement an entire new way of living that is awe-inspiring, our two other siblings would soon follow suit with witness of our new found life. But upon finishing the book, I felt differently than David, even though it was a feel good read, I just felt a fictitious element to it that didn't resonate a realistic diagram for a new way of life. I remember when the buzz and popularity of that particular book subsided; there was no sizable change in my brother, his friends, or anyone that I knew that read it.

Conversely, when the other book emerged in my thirties, it hugely inspired me. It was given to me by a friend that was so motivated that she bought copies for all of her friends. The book's basic premise was that anything you can believe you will possess with one hundred percent certainty you will have. It gave a method by which you change your behaviors to completely act as if you have already received your request. I believe one of the examples was if you were single and had always wanted to be married, you should clean out one side of the closet for your new mate and make plans for the two of you. The book also explained that because your thoughts produce what your thoughts incur, that if you worry about something obsessively or even sometimes, you must put those thoughts out of your mind as they will manifest the thing that you worry about. By example, if a person constantly worries about contracting a terminal illness, eventually he or she will, quite literally, become ill.

The book became a national best seller as well as a bestselling movie; a documentary type instructional device about how to have everything your heart desires. It depicted a child wanting a bicycle and exuding so much belief that the boy opens the door and a bike is on his front porch.

I loved this book as well as the movie. After all, this was something I could do. I've always been a bit gullible and persuasive; the perfect candidate for hypnosis and perhaps the perfect victim for a Ponzi scheme. I believe everyone at face value and I always have. My kids make fun of this as I am the perfect choice for a practical joke. Believing has always come naturally to me, and I believe that is why I considered this book an easy lifestyle change. But like all motivational books, after I believed wholeheartedly and changes did not manifest, the book went on a shelf.

I do not criticize either of these books as I am sure the authors were well intended and the methodology may work for some. Actually, unwavering belief and streamlining your thoughts into words into manifestation is a huge element in receiving the promise. This is discussed in Chapter Ten entitled The Power of The Word. But scientifically and pragmatically, the most important element of change is implementing a new set of rules for living called The Ten Commandments. It's a simple tweak to living. Some find this premise obvious or too "square".

If you think this idea of revisiting the commandments is intended to create a bunch of Bible thumpers and holy rollers, it's not at all. This idea is personal and private and is not intended to convert the average guy into a Christian freak. It's about getting back to basics; it's not about religion.

I put it all to the test; what I'd learned from those books, my favorite spiritual author Emmet Fox, Ernest Holmes and many others. They all evoke this premise of this practice. I can say with complete clarity that believing something into fruition or worrying something into manifestation cannot happen by thought alone. When I consider all of the times I was positive a great thing would happen and it didn't, I can resolve this conclusion. Conversely, when I first gave birth to my children, I worried so much about SIDS (sudden infant death syndrome) that I didn't sleep well for constantly checking on my infants. It never happened.

The change can only be obtained through the observance of the importance of His belief system; not ours. This mindset, coupled with the facets of faith, is when change is eminent.

These basic guidelines for living are pretty straight forth and reasonable. They do not require a huge lifestyle transformation. It's a modification; a simple revision. The commandments don't say that we cannot party down at The Super Bowl, or have sex with a consenting stranger, or be a nudist. They are simply the ten requirements that God asked of us.

Forget the notion that sacrifice and mediocrity is pleasing to God; that's ridiculous. God's inheritance boasts "all of the land", not a small, corner lot! In virtually every verse in scripture quoted of God or Jesus; receiving the promise of abundance, health, and happiness is PREFACED with living by His rules.

Ten examples of a specific blueprint to obtainment…

Exodus 15:26

And said, Of thou wilt diligently hearken to the voice of the Lord thy God, and wilt do that which is right in his sight, and wilt give ear to His commandments, and keep all his statutes, I will put none of these diseases upon thee, which I have brought upon the Egyptians: for I am the Lord that healeth thee.

…

Leviticus 26:3/6

If ye walk in my statutes, and keep my commandments, and do them; Then I will give you rain in due season, and the land shall yield her increase, and the trees of the field shall yield their fruit. And I will give peace in the land, and ye shall lie down, and none shall make you afraid...

...

Deuteronomy 6:6-10

And these words, which I command thee this day, shall be in thine heart: And thou shalt teach them diligently unto thy children, and shalt talk of them when thou sittest in thine house, and when thou when thou walkest by the way...to give thee great and goodly cities, which thou buildest not, and wells digged, which thou diggest not, vineyards and olive trees, which thou plantest not, when thou shalt have eaten and be full.

...

First Kings 11:38

Keep my statutes and my commandments, as David my servant did, that I will be with thee, and build thee a sure house, as I built for David, and will give Israel unto thee. (in scripture, the term "Israel" is symbolic of every good thing life has to offer)

...

First Chronicles 28:8

...keep and seek for all the commandments of the LORD your God: that ye may possess this good land, and leave it for an inheritance for your children after you forever.

...

Psalms 37:9

For evil doers shall be cut off; but those that wait upon the Lord; they shall inherit the Earth (an inheritance on Earth as opposed to Heaven is receipt of the now)

...

Proverbs 3:1

My son, forget not my law; but let thine heart keep my commandments: For length of days and long life and peace, shall they add to thee.

...

Matthew 6:33

But seek ye first the kingdom of God, and his righteousness (follow His Commandments), and all of these things shall be added onto you.

First John 3:22

And whatsoever we ask; we receive of him, because we keep his commandments

---

And...

Revelations 22:14

Blessed are they that do His commandments that they may have right to the tree of life (the tree of life is all that there is that is good)

Ten specific examples of what we will receive and how we shall receive it; a great way to start or finish every day is to simply read these and the other beautifully stated promises. It is not necessary to dwell on the darkness of The Bible; the perils of repercussions for our sins. Let our journey begin by just being a good follower and the rest will take care of itself.

Whenever asked what was the defining practice or behaviors that lead me to change and the fulfilling life I have today, I say it was revisiting the commandments. I had built a great foundation and relationship with God, I felt I had remained faithful through the hard times, and I had begun loving others well; but it was when I got back to the very core of what I could see God asked of me **and** I implemented it, that the universe opened her doors and I felt the life I feel today. I'm not perfect, not by a long shot (!), and I make mistakes every day, but I do my very best to live within His requirements and as close to Him as I can possibly be.

As you read over the next chapters, remember everyone is different and what I struggled with, you may not, it may already be something you practice. But the best way to remember to implement new behaviors is to read over them every day, just for a moment, so that the practices become permanent. Therefore, whenever you see something relevant in this book, The Bible, or any other book, highlight it so that when you "skim" through it upon completion of the read, you remember your favorite parts, behaviors you need to modify, and practices you'd like to remember to implement. If you are on an iPad or tablet, there are alternate programs you may use, such as PDF Notes, that allow highlighting.

Psalm 112

*Praise ye the LORD, Blessed is the man (**you**) that feareth the Lord; that delighteth greatly in His commandments. His seed (**you**) shall be mighty upon earth: the generations of the upright (**you**) shall be blessed. Wealth and riches in his (**your**) house and his (**your**) righteousness shall endure forever...*

DIAGRAM TO THE DREAM

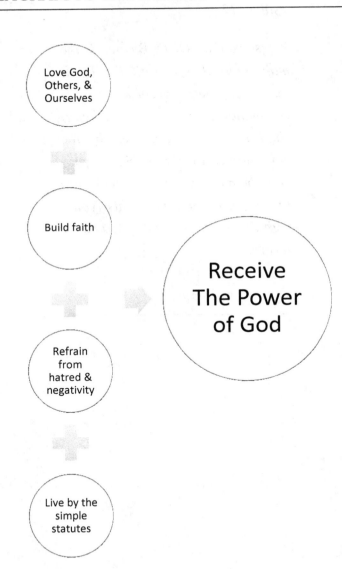

The diagram for living our dream lies in this graph. It's not a secret only handed down to the chosen. We are chosen the moment we set one foot on the path.

Joggers know when they jog a long distance that the last mile is the easiest. One would think that it would be the hardest; that the legs would be exhausted and the lungs tired. But there is a natural ease of the last mile called "the runners high" that enables the last mile to be the fastest.

The same is true of the journey to faith. Once we modify our heart and behavior to live according to His rules, the next step, faith, comes easier because of the accomplishment of the first step. Once we are living and loving in faith, there is a natural absence of hatred, jealousy, and vengeance thus making the last mile the easiest.

James 3:11/12

Doth a fountain send forth at the same place sweet and bitter water?

We cannot be all loving but have hatred for just one select person that wronged us. Just as we cannot believe that God delivered every promise He ever made EXCEPT the promise He made to us. God promised us all of the desires of our heart. If we doubt that God will deliver His promise to us than we believe that God lied.

Therefore, just as a fountain cannot deliver both sweet and bitter water, it is impossible to believe AND doubt.

Deuteronomy 7:12-13

Wherefore it shall come to pass, if ye hearken to these judgments (in reference to His commandments) and keep them and do them, that the Lord Thy God shall keep unto thee the covenant and the mercy which He sware unto thy fathers: And He will love thee and bless thee and multiply thee, He will also bless the fruit of thy womb, and the fruit of thy land, thy corn, and thy wine, and thine oil, the increase of thy kine, and the flocks of thy sheep, in the land which He sware unto thy fathers to give thee.

There is no better promise than His! The 2013 modern day translation is simply that you and your children will have an abundance of all that life has to offer. Why in the world would we live any other way?!

When living according to His commandments, we thus have obtained faith, and as a result have omitted the negatives. We now enter a state of peace and poise. When we find ourselves in this particular state, we receive The Power. The Power is simply the reward of our conscious effort to first seek and then implement with the essence of patience.

CHAPTER 2} DISCERN FOR YOURSELF

Our entire journey depends on the sole intellect of the greatest interpreter of scripture that God placed upon this earth. There is only one person in the world that holds all of the true facets of how to live with faith in God. It is our responsibility to God to only listen to the expert and follow his or her way. Our entire life and existence holds within the balance of his or her knowledge and discernment of scripture. That person is you.

Think about it. If our entire life on earth and our everlasting existence hinges on living as God ask of us; why would we entrust anyone besides ourselves to discern His requirements?

If our spirit's entire journey is placed in the hands of what we learn from seven hundred great sermons from our pastor, attending Mass or Church, three or four inspirational books we've read, and a few great faith seminars we've attended; have we done the work that God asked of us?

All of these entities are wonderful ways to encourage our faith and learn scripture. But until we read God's word for ourselves to determine His expectations, we are not following His rules, just another man's interpretation. **Seek and ye shall find. Seek the kingdom. Seek.**

This book will beg the question, has everything I have been taught about The Bible been an unintentional misunderstanding? Are parts that I have been lessoned true yet others false? Does The Bible contain all relevant scripture?

When we look at its many versions as well as the contents, we must remember that man chose the contents and man gave his interpretation. Our work in seeking is to choose which books **we** feel relevant and how **we** determine is the correct way to live.

In December of the year 1945, two Arab peasants stumbled upon one of the most astonishing archaeological discoveries in biblical history. In the city of Nag Hammadi located in Northern Egypt, as two brothers rummaged through the ancient caves in search of fertilizer, they came across a red earthenware jar, nearly a meter tall. The pottery contained thirteen papyrus books bound in leather. Rumors and innuendos surrounded the discovery; perhaps because the brothers did not come forth with the findings immediately. As parts and fragments of their discovery surfaced through the black market, the interest was raised by legitimate officials as to what exactly the brothers had found.

Some thirty years later, the discoverer confessed the details of the discovery. He relayed the reason he and his brother did not go to authorities. They had avenged the death of their father by killing his murderer. Fearing the police investigators would find the books, they asked a priest nearby to hold the books for safekeeping.

Through a highly dramatic series of events, most of the books were sold through the black market and antiquities dealers throughout Egypt. One of the books was sold and found its way to America. Once the Egyptian government learned of the books, an investigation led to the confiscation of the books by the government. They were then deposited to the Coptic Museum in Cairo.

The finder later admitted that many of the pages were lost or thrown away. He said that his mother had even burned many of the pages for warmth not understanding their worth. But what remained was astonishing; fifty two texts including a collection of early Christian gospels such as The Secret Book of James, The Letter of Peter to Phillip, The Gospel of Phillip and The Gospel of Thomas.

As experts raveled through the vast documents, it soon became clear they were Coptic (the current stage of Egyptian language) translations made over 1500 years ago. Fragments of the original documents were found as well written in Greek, the original language of The New Testament. An original portion of The Gospel of Thomas was one of the fragments; with a complete Coptic translation. There is no debate amongst the examiners as to the dating of the manuscripts; the papyrus used as well as the leather bindings date to roughly 350 to 400 years after Jesus died. But the original fragments are argued from 120 A.D to much earlier.

Roughly two years later, an even greater discovery occurred near the shores of The Dead Sea; now referred to as The Dead Sea Scrolls. These ancient texts discovered near the northwest shore contain a collection of 972 texts, some dating over 100 years before Christ! The texts are of huge historical and religious significance because some of the manuscripts are the identical books currently found in The Old Testament. But more fascinating were the discovered texts that were omitted from The Bible. Some of the books, such as The Book of Enoch, were never given a canonized place within The Bible.

We must remember that the versions of The Bible that we read today were put together by committee based on a need to know basis; what Constantine and his appointees thought we needed to know.

We serve an amazing God. Life is a mystery that can only be unraveled with the information given at the time. It is an insult to believe that these findings were an accident, they just happened to be hidden for thousands of years. God intended the discovery of these factual documents in the 1940s for only one intention; He wanted to give validation to the scripture and His laws in a time frame that you and I can trust. We are human. We have doubts to that which we cannot relate. We begin to doubt the integrity of The Book of Genesis because the story has been interpreted and rewritten a thousand times and originated thousands of years ago.

God knows us. He understands we can relate to discoveries in the forties. Many of us were born in the forties or have parents or grandparents born in the forties. We can feel safe knowing that original copies of The Gospel of Thomas were discovered in this generation and interpreted by scholars that are still alive today. That is great news! I have no doubt that in 2145 or 2188 new discoveries will be found again to encourage a new generation. This is how He works!

There is no debating the authenticity of either of the findings; experts agree the scrolls are as ancient as originally presumed. But many debates circle the content of the findings. The Dead Sea Scrolls produced an entire gospel of Isaiah, found in The Bible, and therefore deemed relevant. It also produced The Book of Enoch, not found in The Bible, but argued by many as a relevant discovery as Enoch's name is found in Genesis as the son of Cain.

In the Nag Hammadi scrolls, The Gospel of Thomas was found, but of course there in no Gospel of Thomas in The Bible. Its validity is argued because after Jesus died, it is said that many wrote their own story and attached one of the apostle's names to it to press their own agenda. This argument rings untrue because The Gospel of Thomas delivers the same stories, quotes, and facts found in The Gospels of Paul, Mark, Matthew, and John. Since the premise is not pushing another agenda, it stands to reason that Thomas' gospel is as relevant as the other books.

Further, apostles such as James and Thomas actually walked, talked, and lived with Jesus, whereas Paul did not. Yet Paul's work was chosen to represent over half of The New Testament. Not to discount Paul's great works, but if I wanted to hear what was said in the huddle, I'd prefer hearing it from the quarterback not the fan.

Thomas knew Jesus well. In reading The Gospel of Thomas, this is evident. He quotes Jesus just as James and John do. These men that knew Jesus personally quote him just as two or three friends quote a dearly beloved friend whom they've recently lost, the words may not be identical but in close proximity.

Enoch is a prominent figure in scripture as a direct descendant of Adam and Eve, born of Cain. He is written in Genesis, Hebrews, and even Luke and is said to have lived for 365 years and to have walked with God. Those noted as walking with God all hold prominent roles in scripture. Yet Enoch's Book, available and accessible during the canonization of the books, was deliberately omitted from The Bible.

As humans, we typically refrain from mentioning a detail or event for two main reasons; the detail is insignificant and doesn't warrant attention, or the event doesn't serve our cause. We deliberately withhold information that doesn't serve our purpose.

In reading the findings of each of these discoveries myself, I found many pieces to the puzzle that resonate peace of the wisdom God intended.

For example, The Book of Enoch reveals a different account of earth's creation by which God employed ten thousand angels; each with a specific responsibility. He refers to these angels as figureheads of specific elements, naming an angel named Buddha as the angel of righteousness. Were portions or fragments of this book the inspiration for Buddhism?

The most significant point in these two discoveries is the realization that we were not given all of the information we need for faith within the confines of The Bible. We must trust that parts are missing; thus the need for trust in God.

THE PEACE COMPASS

Before we begin the diagram, let's discuss one important facet by which we ascertain fact from fiction. It is critical to any man on the journey of faith to discern for HIMSELF the validity and relativity of scripture, sermons, speeches, books, and any other material or source.

The peace to decide the truth…

A wise Catholic counselor once gave me a potent and powerful piece of advice that I have never forgotten. I can honestly say I use it every day.

I was struggling with the decision of divorce and was seeing him weekly. Each week, for several weeks, I would flip flop on my decision. One week I would sternly tell him with conviction that I am staying married regardless of the circumstances for the sake of the children; they will be happier with married parents. The following week I would say, with just as much certainty that I am divorcing. I would contradict the week before by saying I am doing this for the sake of my happiness; and the children will be happier in a peaceful home. After many weeks of continual frustration, I asked the counselor whether or not I should divorce. He said, of course, that he could not make a decision like that for me; that only I could make that choice.

I looked at him and said "but it is so hard, it is such a huge decision". His response angered me. I remember him saying "actually, it is quite easy". I was so mad. I thought; how could he minimize my life by saying the decision of divorce is easy? But his next words, in 15 years, I have never forgotten. He said "God always grants us peace for the right decision".

Honestly, the first perfect peace I had felt in months came from that one sentence.

Only the peace God places in our spirit when a thought is placed in our mind, does our body relax with the calmness of truth. From that day forward, I didn't have all the answers, I still don't, but I learned one important answer. And I use it every day, in all that I do, knowing that it is true. I was able to divorce knowing it was the right thing to do. The bonus of the advice given that day is that there is a profound peace in knowing that God can guide us to truth by the feeling we receive within.

What about when you read something; the newspaper, an article about a current celebrity, a definition in Webster's, an autobiography, or even The Bible, does your peace compass guide you? Doesn't the feeling you get right down in your spirit of either peace or uncertainty separate fact from fiction? Even if you are reading a factual document, if a sentence rings untrue to you, an immediate unbalance occurs.

God stamps his approval upon the right choices, thoughts, actions, words, and ideas by the feeling of peace we have within. Sometimes a "factual document" has a flaw. This is why we must do the work. Therefore, we must use our peace compass always and often. God will never steer us wrong.

The biggest primary example of a flawed document is The Book of Genesis. How ironic that the very first book of The Bible is the first time we begin to doubt.

The story of Adam and Eve and the beginning of mankind and the human race doesn't even make sense.

As we begin to read about creation of the human race we understand that God created Adam and Eve. They had Cain and Abel. Cain killed Abel, and then Cain took a wife. This is the precise moment in Sunday school when the hands of the bold anxiously rise and beg the question; where did Cain's wife come from? Was she a sibling? Were other humans created by God and her origins were simply omitted from the book?

There is no answer other than the obvious...The Bible doesn't contain all of the answers. Because of the discoveries at Nag Hammadi and The Dead Sea, what we can say without hesitation is that we were only provided with the information God intended us to know.

Instead of allowing the first book of The Bible to give us doubt, we must understand that we are given only a certain amount of data, instead of doubting we must study the facts at hand and derive our own conclusions.

CHAPTER 3} LOVE GOD FIRST

Faith, prayer, praise, obedience, belief, repentance, and seeking are the seven elements discussed in how we love God first.

Don't let the word obedience intimidate. It simply means following the commandments and the rule of love. Most of us are almost there; we just need a full understanding of the requirements.

Consider each facet and carefully do a self-analysis; inventory what elements you must change. Consider behaviors you need help with and bring them to prayer. Remember, true change of self can only be accomplished through divine transformation.

FAITH

I think looking back on my journey in faith thus far; I confused the word faith for the word belief. I struggled for years thinking...I just don't get it. I believe, I believe, I believe; I don't understand why I don't feel as if I have a true relationship with God.

I had such an anxiety; as if I were trying to put an entire puzzle together knowing I didn't have all of the pieces. I remember feeling this way:

✓ I feel so far away from God

- ✓ My prayers aren't really answered; well maybe sometimes
- ✓ I'm doing all the right things, I attend church, I tithe, I volunteer, I pray
- ✓ I'm always struggling with something; work, finances, my health, my marriage
- ✓ If God loves me, why doesn't He bless me and help me

What always struck me about priests and nuns was their ability to, most of them, at a very young age; give their entire life to God. Especially as a Catholic school girl. My dream was to become a mom, hopefully as good of a mom as my mom. I imagined that most of these priests and nuns had also been raised attending Catholic schools with loving parents that loved them as much as my parents loved me.

As a teenager as well as adult, it was absolutely inconceivable to me to make a commitment to never have a family and thus give my life to serving God. I remember an evening about fifteen years ago when a Catholic priest walked me to my car. At the time, I was serving on five different church committees as well as attending mass every Sunday.

But I was just a robot doing what I thought I needed to do. I thought the person to ask about true faith is a nun or priest. It was with this mindset that I HAD to ask him the question; "Father, where do you get faith, I mean, how *do* you get it, how *did* you get it? I don't even remember his response but I think it was something like, "oh it takes time but I'm sure you have more than you know." The answer he gave was kind, but I knew he was wrong. At the very least, I knew I had little faith. I knew I believed in God, and I knew that people thought I was "religious", but I knew that I just didn't have it. Whatever "it" was.

I believe my journey to fiG (faith in God) began when I started reading books about faith and spirituality. After reading everything from Fox, I began to read anything I could get my hands on. I would read two or three chapters and discover a feeling of uncertainty or even distress...just God's way of giving me a nudge that I was not on the right path. I would put that book down and begin another.

The definition of love is a peace in the spirit birthed by joy, bliss, and concern for another ABSENT of jealousy, vengeance, hatred, malice, or judgment. It is pure therefore void of any negative. Love God before all else, love thy neighbor as thyself and be full of self-love. Jesus expressed these three requirements in His time on Earth more than any other law of God. Its importance is the very essence of faith.

When ascertaining the quintessence of loving God first, let us look at the definition of "love" outlined above and add before the word "concern", the word **ultimate.**

In my research and thirst for wisdom, I stumbled upon a book by Paul Tillich called The Dynamics of Faith. His definition of faith resonated peace so deeply within my spirit that I knew it was right. My peace compass jumped with accuracy. The definition he gave for faith absolutely changed my life. It enabled me the understanding of the word that in turn gave me simple instruction that started me on the right path.

In essence, he defines faith as having ultimate concern for God. Further, "ultimate concern" he explains, is simply thinking about God all of the time. Faith means including God in our decisions and in all of the small and large places in our life. Finally, I understood. I was so excited! I now conclusively not only knew the true meaning of faith, I had already begun implementing the premise.

With understanding its true definition; I now love the word faith, and "in God" is the two words that naturally follow. It is only in God that faith is necessary. Again, not mistaking the word belief for faith, is there anything in the world that we should have faith in other than God? To give ultimate and complete concern to family, job, children, friends, money, vacations, possessions, dating, politics or any other earthly thing defeats the true purpose of living.

Little by little, I began to pray. I began to pray more. Eventually, as our relationship grew, I realized I was building concern with God. I once heard a very inspirational woman on television say "God is not offended if you ask him for the best parking spot, he knows you don't mind walking, he's glad you asked because you are letting Him into your world". I thought that was very well put and accurate. God pleasures in His children asking for help…in things great and small. And as His daughter, I really do get some pretty good parking spots.

I was confusing the word faith with belief. I did not have faith. I simply did not have it. Faith is praying, loving, and talking to God every day, all the time, until it is as natural as breathing. Faith is thinking about God in every situation and especially every decision. It is not a job. It is not a chore. It is not a discipline. It is not even time consuming. It's simple, easy, and natural. And the best thing is, once you practice and successfully live it, it is the most wonderful relationship you will ever have!

PRAYER

A theory exists that people develop and mold their relationship with God similarly to the relationship they have or had with their earthly father. Theoretically, the person will establish the way in which they pray similar to how they talk to their dad.

For me, it seemed a fair analysis. My dad lives about 700 miles from me. Until recent years, I only called him maybe once a month or even every other month. If I talked with him more than that, it was indirectly through a phone call with my mom, in which he'd get on the line briefly.

I never asked my dad for much because I knew that he loved me but historically he's never really been the "go to" guy for me. If I needed anything, I would call my mom. Coincidentally, until recent years that would also describe my relationship with God. I only talked to God when I thought I had to. Prayer was sporadic, uncomfortable, impersonal, and insincere. Thankfully, when my relationship with God transformed; so did my relationship with my dad. Not surprisingly, all of my relationships are better.

Growing up Catholic, we prayed the rosary. When I say "we" I actually mean "they" in that whatever I was doing, it definitely wasn't praying. It was more like mindless chanting. I don't think I ever thought of the words that I was saying even once. More importantly, when I came away from prayer, I came away unchanged. I am positive God did not hear my mindless chanting. I'm sure he felt my effort.

When to pray…

If I were to build a new relationship with my earthly father, which scenario would cultivate a sincere rapport? Suppose because my dad lives in Alabama, I decided to call him absolutely every day at ten a.m. and speak for fifteen minutes. Suppose I make a pact with myself that even though I am a single parent of five and work full time, I will not falter from calling him at that precise time.

On the other hand, consider that instead of calling him every day at ten, I called him several times a day and asked his opinion on the things I know he can answer, or simply said "I just saw an awesome golf course and thought about you", or "your granddaughter just did the cutest thing and I wanted to tell you about it real quick". I reason that he would feel more sincerity from spontaneity verses scheduled calls.

If we visit spontaneously with God in earnest sincerity and allow Him into our life, like most earthly fathers, He will love and support us for all of our days.

In lieu of praying at precisely seven, noon, and nine with the same prayer; try talking to Him impulsively. You will be amazed at how quickly you will establish a true bond. Further, you will begin to understand the true essence of the phrase "you are never alone", and truly and for the first time, He is with you as Father and child.

There should be no difference to the tone of your voice or the words that you choose. Once I began praying and said "God thank you so much for all of the gifts you have bestowed on me." I immediately began to laugh and then clarified with… "Father, I don't know where that came from; you know I never use the word bestowed!" He knows you; speak to Him in the same fashion you would speak to any loved one. There is no need to stand on ceremony. He loves you. He knows you and He knows the desires of your heart.

How to pray…

It is so important to pray sincerely and from the heart. In Matthew we are warned not to pray repetitiously. We are also given by Jesus the perfect prayer, The Lord's Prayer. It is a beautiful and inspiring example of how to pray. Emmet Fox gives an analysis of the prayer in The Sermon on the Mount, dissecting each line and why it was written with such handpicked and carefully chosen words. He gives an amazing interpretation of why Jesus chose every term with precision and intention.

This is a good way to begin prayer or to end it. We must use care and say the prayer once, one line at a time, focusing on each word as an honest devotion to our Father. It is not necessary that we pray it daily. It's important to be true to God. He knows what we are thinking.

The God we serve doesn't care if we are dreaming about a big house or wish we would find a husband or get a better job. Our God wants us to say what is on our minds. Therefore, if we sit down for a little prayer time and can't think of a thing to say, start with The Lord's Prayer. If there is something troubling us, God is the first place to visit. God knows our needs.

God is our best friend, brother, sister, teacher, father and mother encompassed as one. He does not judge us when we fail, make a mistake, or sin. Anything brought in prayer will be answered to those who believe. He will only pleasure in our success. When we honor God and praise him daily, our blessings will be abundant.

My prayers are hugely informal…

My father, I just love you so much. Thank you, thank you so much for the incredible weather yesterday. I can't believe how awesome the temperature was and how beautiful the sky was. It just made Julia's tournament so enjoyable. God, I forgot to tell you yesterday thanks for the blessing of being able to buy whatever I wanted for the kids and me at the grocery store. God, I'm so happy how well I handled the kids when they got into the big fight. I didn't lose my cool once and I thank you for helping me with that. Father, every day is beautiful for me, I'm so happy for every single blessing you've given me...my beautiful home, my car is still running, my awesome kids. Not in that order, of course. But you know that and you know what is important to me. God, I ask you to help me with the bills. I don't want to work hard all the time. I want financial security and abundance. I want to not worry about supporting the kids. I want to prosper so that I can be worry free. You know that I have always been sad about people who are hurting in any way and especially people without homes. God, please allow me to prosper not only for myself but also to help others. Oh my goodness...I just love you so much and feel your love absolutely every minute of every day. Talk to you more in a bit...love ya

That is a very impromptu and unedited example. God loves me and knows I am informal. Why would I pretend to be someone I'm not with My Creator? Not gonna fool him and he loves me just the way I am...He better! He made me. It feels incredible as a mom who gives love all day to feel His unconditional love given to me.

Another implementation of praying is trust in His word and His promise. There is a natural tendency when we present a request to God to be repetitious; asking for the same thing every day. This is natural because as humans we demand answers. When we request something from someone on earth, we at the very least require a yes or no response. Because our relationship with God involves ultimate belief and faith, we must ask ONLY ONCE. We must not beg. It tells God we are unsure of His power.

Imagine how it makes God feel when we beg. Think about it. God PROMISED us that when we live in faith, He will provide us with EVERYTHING. He never said WHEN. If He indicated when, there would be no need of faith.

Imagine hypothetically you found yourself in financial difficulty. Suppose your parents had agreed to a loan. They gave you their word. They indicated that they are receiving a tax refund in two months and you may have it.

What if the very next day, you called your dad and said "Dad, it is critical that I have that money, are you still going to loan it to me?" How do you think that would make him feel? What if you waited three more days and called him again and said "Dad, please, please, help me, they are going to foreclose on my house if you don't help me". Your dad would feel terribly. Your parents would know you didn't trust them.

God WILL answer our prayers, but only when He is certain we are ready. THE BEST WAY TO BE READY IS TRUST. TRUST HIM. If we are destitute…TRUST HIM. If we are extremely ill…DON'T STOP TRUSTING HIM. If we are lonely…TRUST HIM. The answer will come when the work in us is complete.

When my kids ask questions like "Mom, why do we get the flu?" or this past summer in St. Louis "why is there a heat advisory, why can't we play outside again today?" My answer is this. If we were never sick a day in our lives, we could not possibly be thankful for healthy days. If there were not heat advisories and bitter cold days, it would be an impossibility to be thankful for gorgeous 75 degree days.

Think about it. People who live in Southern California never walk outside and say "God thank you so much that it is not bitter cold today". Additionally, people who are rarely sick seldom give thanks for another well day. I ponder if the most faithful man who has never encountered the flu gives thanks daily for another well day.

Consequently, if we have not experienced poverty or financial struggles, it is very difficult to be thankful for the ability to partake in "extras'. I often wonder if the royal family gives daily thanks for the money to buy groceries and to go on vacation. If they do, that is indeed impressive.

My daughter watches a show about a popular brother's musical group in which one of the brothers is married. It is their marriage and the life of this couple that is the shows focus. The brothers group is very successful and prosperous. Their parents managed them to become one of the most lucrative bands of today. But they started out as just a normal, middle class family.

In one episode, the brothers are just about to go on stage and the family is hustling and bustling about in hurriedness before they go on. The dad, in the mist of the turmoil, REQUIRES everyone to drop what they are doing and listen to him. As he gathers them in a business fashion, he calmly bows his head and begins to pray. The other family members bow their heads as well. He gives thanks. It is evident at this point that this is not only a ritual before performance, but a value instilled long before fame and fortune.

As he begins in prayer, he immediately thanks God; giving Him credit for absolutely all of their accomplishments, wealth, blessings, and success. Here is a family that knows that while they are smart and talented, they know Who provided all. Now I enjoy watching the show, it's so nice to see a family living in faith. Remember when we send up thankfulness, He rains down abundance.

Always pray for exactly what you want. God has a limitless supply and is not at all offended. If you want to be the next PGA Champion of the World **and** you live in faith; you will be just that. If you want to be a billionaire; **and** you live in faith you will be just that. If you want to be the best mom and wife and live happily ever after **and** you live in faith; you will be just that. God not only knows what your heart wants, He is excited about giving it to you. But it's up to you to **ask** for it **and** live in faith.

When we are absolutely too busy to pray, this is the day we must pray longer. This rule, I have found, is truly golden. On the days that I have taken more time to talk to God, I can statistically report that life runs much more smoothly.

I can say without hesitation that every time I have asked God for the right words to say in an important situation, I have had better results than I could have imagined. When you have faith in our awesome God, *there is a quiet and confident peace that cannot be given by anyone or anything else.* When you stay in faith, He will take care of you.

Another way to pray is by meditation. Sometimes our problems are so great that they become overwhelming and too huge to even talk about with God. Please remember that God knows what we need before we know it ourselves. Therefore, the best way to ask for what we need is to simply meditate and focus on God. Just think long and hard about every good thing you can think of about God. Next, think of all of your blessings. Finally, we must be still and listen to what it is that He would like us to know.

PRAISE

An additional essential element to prayer is praise. Once we are living in His favor and following His divine guidance, we have achieved faith. When we have achieved faith, there is a magical transformation that occurs with praise.

God pleasures in seeing His children use the gifts He gave. God gave us the Power of Praise. Praise is giving God thanks for all that He has given. *The Power of Praise is the act of taking the spoken word and empowering that which is said into that which shall be.*

When we give thanks for our requests before we receive, it demonstrates the power of our unwavering belief.

As I sat alone within the four walls of my bedroom writing, I knew God wanted me to write. I also knew within my spirit that I would be able to do what I loved to do and make a living doing it. But after I published my first book and it didn't provide enough income to support me, I began to wonder if I had misinterpreted God's destiny for me.

I wondered if I could've been foolish enough to believe that I could be a writer. It was not until I enacted The Power of Praise that my dream came to pass. The mistake lied in "I wonder". Wonder is another word for doubt. The moment we doubt the dream is the moment the dream is placed on hold.

Without one book sold, I knew I would sell over a million copies; a record of a book in this genre. I took a new approach:

God, thank you that I am now a successful writer. Thank you that I can now support myself, my kids, and have enough to help others. God, I love you so very much.

Doubt will get you nowhere fast. Belief will take you to The New York Times Best Seller List.

Sometimes when things are tough, it may be that all you can think of to be thankful of is that you live in a free country, that you have the faculties to be able to pray, that you have your youth, or maybe that you can see, or walk. Vast numbers of the world's population would consider hot and cold running water a huge blessing. Maybe I've touched upon one thing you do not have.

Remember this; when we tell God thank you for what we do have, magic truly begins. Virtually everyone I know who has learned this principle has been blessed in ways they could never imagine. I once heard a talk show personality say that God has a dream for you bigger than you could dream for yourself. I can tell you from my personal experience that an amazing transformation began to occur when I realized the necessity of true praise and a thankful heart.

FOLLOW HIS COMMANDMENTS

You will have no god and serve no god except Me.

You will not take God's name in vain.

You will keep holy The Sabbath Day.

You will not make a false image of Me and worship it.

Honor your mother and your father.

Do not kill.

Do not commit adultery.

Do not steal.

Do not lie about others.

Do not have jealousy in your heart for what belongs to another.

His commandments are self-explanatory. When you look at the list, evaluate specifically in number the amount of commandments you break on a regular basis. Now calculate the number of ones you've broken in the past but now follow.

Are you surprised? This is a difficult portion of the journey. We must be honest with ourselves and immediately cease and discontinue any wrong doing. These laws are very important to Him, so much so that your existence on Earth is hinged on following them.

It isn't necessary for me to dissect each commandment as to its meaning; however, it is critical that you do. We must discern for ourselves through scripture the true meaning of each. It is unlawful to follow another man's interpretation if it doesn't seem accurate to you. There is no harm in being in agreement with someone as long as it brings peace within you.

I would like to offer two thoughts regarding clarification to two commonly misunderstood commandments. God is adamant about The Sabbath Day and it should be a day of rest and relaxation void of working. But Jesus clarifies in The New Testament the exception...things that are necessary. Therefore, we must exercise common sense. Cooking and doing the dishes are essential to feeding the family and therefore would be exempt.

Additionally, professions such as a health care professional or a fire fighter certainly fall into a necessary category. But if you are working on Sunday at a job that is questionable as to necessity, please search your heart for clarity as well as scripture for discernment and act according to your decision.

The second commandment is often misunderstood but valid enough to be listed in the top three. It has a greater importance than to actually create a statue of God or an item of Heaven and worship it. Because God is omnipresent and all knowing, he knew that this rule would be often broken; therefore, we must be clear as to what this statute means and how we must honor it. This commandment tells us that God has only given us the information about Him that He wants us to understand. The remainder of His identity is His intentional mystery. He never elaborates His precise image or gives His exact location or discerns His specific meaning(s). He is limitless. Therefore, the sin lies in creating our own version of Him that is specific to what we like, what we want and what we decide He should be. This may be the most infracted rule in the ten. There are countless people, groups, and yes, even denominations that create "their God" for the explicit intent of their own agenda. Man has lied, cheated, and even killed under his own false god.

I have found another commonly broken commandment regards bearing false witness; commonly referred to as lying. Unfortunately, this is a commandment I found that I was breaking on a regular basis. I thought it was completely harmless to, for example, lie about having a work engagement to avoid a social event or exaggerate how well my first book did to give it more credibility. But the truth is, the moment I instigated true change is when I received true change and success.

I once knew a gentleman who I considered a Godly man. He studied the Bible, as well as just had a kind heart and gentle demeanor. However, he honestly believed it ok to be untruthful in business. He said that scripture supported it; that we should remedy evil with evil and he believed mankind as generally evil. He continually lied about his assets, his capital, his credentials, and even manufactured fake locations globally; He said it gave the business a "larger presence" and the lies didn't hurt anyone. But the lies did hurt others; they were making business decisions based on fiction and he was not able to perform. This man completely lost all of his clients and his business went under; he financially lost everything.

This is an example I think of when I consider bending any of God's rules for my benefit. I know that lying is wrong. Are there exceptions to that rule? Of course, and it is an easy determination. We must use the equation of the three facets of love; does it hurt God, hurt anyone, or hurt ourselves? This is the best guide to determine what is acceptable. Certainly, if a friend has a terminal illness and asks how she looks, the last thing we would say is "you look as if you are close to death". We would give words of encouragement knowing that it is the best thing to do in the moment. Lying about someone, lying for self-gain, or for simplicity in the moment is just wrong.

BELIEVE

I found out that the company I worked for was unable to pay me my substantial commission. The check I had waited patiently for that would sustain the kids and me for six months was not coming. I was devastated. It was June. My plan was to put the proceeds in the bank so that the kids and I would be able to live for the next six months. I had calculated our budget from the prior six months and I knew that even if I did not make another dime until December we would be fine. But my company went under. Not only was I not getting paid, I no longer had a job. To make matters worse, I had conservatively lived on my last bit of savings awaiting this money, which was no longer coming. To add insult to injury, my car had failed emissions and needed two thousand dollars in repairs and I was counting on the commission check to get my expired license plates renewed. I was using the car with expired plates only for basic necessities such as getting groceries and taking the kids only where they had to go. I had been pulled over and received a collection of tickets ranging from expired plates to failure to have insurance as well as no registration.

I found myself with rent due, groceries needed, utility bills, and no income. Worse than no income, I had no car to drive to even go on a job interview. Because of my recent divorce I had lost touch with the handful of friends that I had. My family lived over 700 miles away. I couldn't even borrow a car; I knew no one that could help. My younger kids rode the bus home from school so I didn't have to pick them up but my older children opted to stay with their dad when I couldn't pick them up. This made me very sad but they understood.

So I made up my mind to stay in faith. I decided that if I could not drive then whatever it was that I was to do to keep us in the adorable little house that we were renting must be done within its walls.

I felt compelled to write. I didn't know why exactly but I just started writing. Although I had my idea for what I wanted to write about, I didn't write on that subject. I continued to write about faith. Every day I felt a greater sense of peace that not only was this what I was supposed to write about but that the answer was on the way.

It is an odd yet completely satisfying feeling. It is what scripture describes as entering into the rest. When you are doing what God gives you the energy to do there is an undeniable feeling of clarity. At times I must admit my mind would occasionally start to doubt. I would think "oh my goodness, I can't pay the bills or buy groceries, I have to get a job". But honestly each time a new miracle would occur that encouraged me to stay the course. In the six months that I had earned not a dime, each bill was miraculously paid. I am not exaggerating.

I attempted to sell my car but I couldn't give it away. The selling of it would have been very helpful but God just didn't allow it. Instead, He allowed tiny miracles unmistakable of His work. It happened absolutely every time I was in need.

I friend had given me a Visa Gift Card; unsure of the amount on the card. I was in desperate need of groceries. I went online to all of the local grocery stores to see which ones could deliver groceries. When I found one, I conservatively ordered about sixty dollars in groceries not knowing how much credit the card held. The transaction went through and I immediately burst in to tears. It was Thanksgiving and I had not enough to prepare a single meal, now I could make a great brunch for the kids and me. But after the holiday I again was left with no food for us. I used the card again and this time for one hundred dollars. It went through and I cried again. This happened three more times until I just had plenty.

When I realized I had enough groceries to last me quite a while I received a phone call from the grocery store. She said that she had no idea why their system allowed the credit card to go through because there was only ten dollars on the card. I apologized and told her I was financially strapped and would pay the balance just as soon as I could. She later called and said that it was their mistake and not to worry about the bill, they had already taken care of it. Another miracle! These type of occurrences never happened to me prior to my journey to faith.

When Christmas arrived, I had not a penny to my name. My parents came into town and lent me the little they had for a few gifts for the kids. I had listed all of the furniture, games, and items the kids and I no longer used for sale. Like clockwork I would get a phone call that not only was someone interested in the item but they would quickly come to purchase it.

My cell phone was the only phone we had. I could not afford it. You know how cell phone companies are; if they say they are suspending your service for non-payment on the first, you will have no service after midnight on the thirty first! My service was only disconnected once. Miraculously, I received a small amount of cash to reinstate the service. After that, it was never suspended again. Every day I thanked God for another day.

After that, I knew to trust God. Whenever I began to worry, I remembered Jesus' words to His disciples. He was so exasperated with the fact that they had seen Him perform so many miracles yet still questioned his ability. They often felt compelled to ask Him when problems occurred, how they would be resolved. This upset Jesus. He said "oh ye of little faith" because he was angered of their obvious uncertainty and lack of faith.

I had seen Him provide heat, electricity, groceries, and a home for me without a cent to my name. Yet I still doubted as did His disciples. It was with this mindset that I stopped doubting. Every time I thought "oh no" I replaced it with "oh ye of little faith". Honestly, I'd seen so many miracles, why in the world would I doubt?

I now know that all of the years that I volunteered countless hours at my church, took my children to church every Sunday, believed in God and tried to be a good mom and person that I was not living in faith. The irony is that the way I lived before was much harder in comparison to the way I live today. It required so much effort. I will never stop thanking God for clearing the path for me for a better understanding of how to live fulfilled with His promises. It is easy and once you get it, you just get it. Then you begin to live.

REPENTANCE

Be sorry and mean it. Often we apologize; but we don't mean it. Some of us never apologize. Sometimes we apologize earnestly and are genuinely sorry for our actions, only to repeat that same action again. Being truly apologetic is evidentially supported by the conscious effort to abstain from the same action. Of course we are all repeat offenders, but we must make daily commitments of self-betterment. This is how God and others know we are, in fact, regretful.

Every day we must offer to God repentance for our sins. It doesn't have to be formal, it is not necessary to kneel or be in a church. It is necessary to do two things; confess the sin aloud to God and pray sincerely for the ability to change the behavior.

Example:

Father, I am so sorry for the ugliness I felt about my ex-husband this morning. He makes me so angry that I begin to wish he will have some sort of misfortune. It was so wrong and in my heart now I love him again. God, please help me to react better when he and I quarrel.

Father, I am sorry I gossiped about Jen last night. I know that it is wrong; I just wanted to be part of the group. I should've excused myself. Please help me be a better person. Please help me refrain from gossip.

God knows we are not perfect, and he forgave us the moment we sinned. But scripture tells us to repent. It is God's love for us reflected in this rule. Because the spoken word holds so much power, it enables us the ability to understand our error and grow spiritually. It is part of the transformation that ultimately leads us to the victory in store.

SEEK

It is imperative that we begin a new life today within the commandments as opposed to later. Why wait? Many wait because they believe living in faith means giving up fun. This is a ridiculous notion built upon a foundation of agendas and misconceptions passed on from generation to generation. The truth is God wants us to pleasure in the gifts He gave. If He didn't, why would he have designed us to derive it?

I remember knowing certain kids in high school that I considered "goody two shoes". I'm sure you remember one, or perhaps you were one. What I remember about them is that I thought they were no fun and that they were having no fun. I was having a blast in high school.

Part of loving God is seeking what He wants of us.

I used to think to myself…gosh, I'm Catholic, I believe in Jesus, I will be a good Christian someday but not right now; I want to have fun. That was just one of my many misconceptions regarding faith. I thought I could not live in faith AND have fun. God wouldn't have cared about ANY of the things I did in high school. Unfortunately, society taught me that if I drank and had fun at parties, I could not simultaneously have a close relationship with God. My parents convinced me what their parents convinced them of. What a shame to have wasted all of those years not walking in faith because of words spoken by man.

The injustice is that this is how relationships with God are severed. There are many good and faithful parents that raise their children to love The Lord. Often times, the child that was nurtured in faith will stray from God as a teenager. He will operate under the misconception that if he has sex or drinks alcohol he is dishonoring God. We can have faith in God and still be ourselves. We must never pause or stop living in faith just because of a misstep or poor choice. Often, what we consider sinful because of our upbringing, God does not. If we have sinned, this is when we need God most.

It is NOT a sin to drink alcohol, have sex, masturbate, smoke cigarettes, smoke marijuana or use drugs. Of all of the entities on that list NOT ONE of them are prohibited by God. God considers **over indulgence** sinful because it is hurtful to us. Drug use and marijuana is against the law of man and common sense tells us to refrain. We have to live within the confines of our national and local laws to avoid the consequences such as prison. Often times because some of the laws of God and the laws of man(stealing and killing for example) are the same, we confuse God's laws for man's.

I think the most important question to ask oneself in gauging right from wrong is this: Do my actions hurt My God, my neighbor or myself? ALL of the commandments and requirements of us from Our Father are derived from this. God knows that it is an impossibility to live on this earth in a joyful way without His love, guidance, and favor.

Therefore, the first two commandments are of Him. The third commandment tells us to keep holy the Sabbath. This day God gave, as much for us, as Him. He wants us to rejuvenate and rest. Just as a parent does not like to see her child working endless hours; our Father wants us to enjoy the earth, family, friends, and feast at least one day of the week. The remaining commandments deal specifically in rules that, when broken, directly affect His children.

Therefore, it is an easy moral gauge to ask oneself the question; does this action that I am doing hurt myself or my fellow man? Therefore, it is imperative to use this equation to decipher right from wrong. I call it the hurt factor. The hurt factor is just the meter of our action's ability to hurt ourselves or someone else.

CHAPTER 4}
MISINTERPRETATIONS OF OUR FOREFATHERS

Seeking what God requires of us is critical, but just is critical is the necessity to explore what we've been taught or subjected to that is simply untrue. Centuries of misconceptions can lead us away from God. Remembering to keep the mind and heart open to correct discernment; let us consider and explore what scripture really says about these important topics.

EVOLUTION VERSES CREATION

This topic has been one of the biggest debates for the absence of God. Ironically, when observing and studying the evolution of man, our progress to the modern man of today can be from nothing other than The Most High Creator of the Universe.

Churches and religious denominations have been their own worst enemy in this regard. Continually teaching that Adam and Eve were the first humans to exist is fine; but science through paleontology and archaeology has created a fair argument for a different scenario.

Scripture doesn't mention dinosaurs, cave men or opposable thumbs. The Big Bang Theory represents a different depiction of creation entirely; giving a timeline of the creation of the entire universe over 13 billion years ago.

Genesis has two opposing stories of the creation of man; one account in which God creates man and woman, and two pages later the story of Adam and Eve. Again, The Bible instills immediate doubt in the minds of the lay biblical reader within the very first book.

It is critical to understand two fundamental truths; the Bible consists of the fragments of creation that God wanted us to know and it is an insult to science and the evolution of mankind to not accept both the **fact** of God's responsibility for creation and the **plausibility** of Big Bang.

Over ninety percent of the human race believes that God created The World, but a diminutive doubt begins to immerge when we hear scientific explanations that may discount the depiction in Genesis. This is how God works. Otherwise, there would be no reason for faith. The important element to remember in faith is to use the peace compass to ascertain a reasonable explanation. We do not have to stare blankly at a cult leader and chant "I believe I believe I believe", like a mindless follower. We simply have to ascertain the reasonable explanation that God did not give all of the facts; He intentionally left mystery for us to seek, ascertain, and continue to believe. He is telling us "those who have eyes to see and ears to hear" have the ability to deduce reasonable conclusions.

The link to evolution and creation is clearly obvious. God is the great I Am, The Constant, The Light, and The Beginning. He created the earth, planets, moon, sun, and stars possibly over thirteen billion years ago. Theories like The Big Bang and Steady State still begin with the abundance of light elements (God created light), atomic and sub-atomic particles such as the first elements hydrogen, helium, and lithium (God created air) and matter (God created the earth).

The Bible says the first man was created from dust(matter). If you believe in The Big Bang Theory you must believe in God! The recipe God used to create The Universe may well be one of these plausible theories but it could not exist without the creation of light, matter, water and atmosphere!

It is only the timeline that throws us. Because The Bible was pounded into our heads as "Adam and Eve were the first"; priests, pastors, and parents are not bold enough to state the obvious. They feel a guilt inherited from past generations that if they do not recognize these two as the very first humans that somehow they have doubted God.

Suppose the two conflicting stories in Genesis conflict because they are giving two different accounts of two different cycles. What if Adam and Eve weren't His first stab at creating man but his first stab at creating thoughtful, free will man? What if depiction number two in Genesis is His prior creation of, for example, cave man or gorillas? What if God has recycled his renditions of creation over and over for over thirteen billion years and we are simply his best work to date? Could it be that Adam and Eve were the first creatures entitled "man" and that his prior prototypes had a different label?

What if Noah's Ark is the first example, known to man, of God saying "I've almost got this right this time, I'm going to keep the current prototype of the physical body by allowing Noah's family to rebuild the population but I'm going to change the mindset of the moral capacity to understand the penalty for dishonoring me?" The abolishment of the population ordered and carried out by God himself with His reason noted as disappointed with his product is a very relevant piece of the puzzle. It's conclusive that a version of man existed that He, upon observance, found subpar.

What if He did the same thing with The Earth? What if he began with the Universe then created the planets and stars alleviating parts of atmosphere to create density and this snowballed to Earth as we know it? These are my humble gatherings, but the important question to ponder is this. Do my theories give you peace, or do you have another conclusion? Most importantly, we must understand that it is ok to believe Genesis **and** believe there was a before. God never said to only believe in the Bible; He said only believe in Him.

I often wonder if this is why The Book of Enoch and other books were destroyed; because they accounted a different version from the already traditionally established beliefs and the priests and church heads feared dissention with the questions that would arise.

CONSUMPTION OF ALCOHOL

It is obvious through the consumption of wine throughout biblical times that it is acceptable and even encouraged. Scripture simply warns us of over-indulgence.

If wine were meant to simply be tasty, why would the alcohol within it loosen our inhibitions and trigger pleasure? If sex was created for the sole intention of procreation, why do we experience an orgasm? Was it His intention to create temptation? Of course not! If that were true, the rules to abstain would be found within the commandments above or below thou shalt not kill.

Drug Use

Because God is all knowing and sees our actions, there is a freedom in His love that we can discuss anything with Him; unlike our earthly parents. Isn't it a beautiful and wonderful feeling to say "Hey Father, I know you know I smoked pot last night at a party. My fear is that I liked it and I may do it again. I don't want to be a pothead; can you help me to not do it again?" When you reach a faithful relationship with God, you will in fact hate marijuana. If he can part the seas as well as create them, he can certainly make the change within you to no longer want to smoke marijuana.

Surgery, Artificial Insemination, and Medicine

I recently heard of a couple that has been trying to have a baby for eight years. She said she really wanted to have invitro fertilization but because she is Catholic, it is their belief that this is a sin. She actually said that she was fearful God would punish her if she had the procedure. I thought of all the people who have successfully had children through this method and have never been "punished".

It reminded me of the story of Abraham and Sarai. Many of us know the story that God had promised them a baby but so many years elapsed that they became too old to conceive. Sarai decided that Abraham should sleep with her maid so that they could help the situation along. The baby was born and they were overjoyed, exclaiming that God had fulfilled His promise; just in an unconventional way. But God corrected them saying that this baby was not from Him and they had taken matters into their own hands. The son was difficult and hard to raise. God told Hagar, his birth mother, that he would be "wild".

But because God never makes a promise that He doesn't keep, Sara(h) became pregnant and gave birth to Isaac, and he went on to live the greatness God had intended.

The story of Abraham and Sarai may be the source of the invitro sin fallacy. The sin of Abraham and Sarai was doubting the promise of God. If God were punishing Sarai for birthing a child using her maid, he would have punished Leah and Rachel two generations later. The opposite is true; after Rachel had many children using her maid, God blessed her with healing her barren womb and giving her two children of her own.

If God didn't want us to use artificial means to conceive, then is it a sin to use an artificial hip verses being crippled?

What about heart bypass surgery, if God wants us to die, should we refrain from surgery?

An old joke comes to mind. A man accidentally missteps next to a strong river and falls into the water. He struggles to stay afloat as the current overcomes him. A man passes next to him in a boat and calls to him "sir, let me give you a hand, I'll pull you into the boat". The man answers 'no thanks, I am a man of faith, God will save me". Another boat comes along and the boater offers help. The man says again "no thank you, God will provide a way", as he struggles to keep his head above water. Finally, the man drowns and goes to heaven. He looks at God and says "Father, I thought you would save me from drowning". God looks at the man perplexed and says "well, I sent two boats!"

Surgery, medication, artificial insemination, and medical help are simply advancements in technology and a sign of the times. Just like the wheel or the telephone, they are inventions by man to enhance our lives. The important question to ask is does this hurt my neighbor, myself or my God? If God didn't want us to use artificial insemination for helping us have a baby would he also not want us to walk with a cane if we are cripple? See the boat joke.

The answer is that these things don't concern God. All of his rules involve loving Him first and loving all humans on earth. The fact of the matter is, the invitro will only be effective if God ordained it so. And more importantly, we will only know whether to use invitro or adoption,etc. through prayer and asking God what to do and getting His peace for the right answer. Through prayer, He may even tell us just to be patient, as He did with Abraham and Sara(h).

BIRTH CONTROL

God created a woman's body to ovulate and produce eggs at a certain time every month. A natural way to have intercourse without conception is to pinpoint the time a woman is not ovulating and simply have intercourse during that time. Catholics refer to this as natural family planning; formerly the rhythm method. But the thought occurs that because God is all-knowing, if He were opposed to birth control, He would have made it evident within the commandments. There would be a prevention of birth commandment.

Additionally, because God created us, if He wanted us to conceive every time we had intercourse, there would be no time slot with the inability to conceive.

We must ask the question does birth control hurt God, my neighbor, or me?

Because scripture does not indicate a rule, I believe that it is completely acceptable to use a contraceptive.

DIVORCE

Is it a sin to divorce? In both testaments divorce is discussed. In the Old Testament, one book relays that if a person is disenchanted or no longer wants to be married, he should simply hand his spouse official divorce papers, and marry someone else. It indicates that the only rule is that the two cannot marry one another again. Paul discusses divorce and marriage. He discourages marriage in the first place because he says it is difficult to serve God first when you have a spouse. He then discusses divorce. What I like about Paul is that he notes that these are his opinions, and they are not of God.

The important thing to remember of both testaments is that God didn't comment on divorce. Jesus specifically indicated that if a man puts away his wife and divorces her, he causes her to commit adultery as well as the man she marries later. He is not, however, condemning divorce. What we know about Jesus is that He would never indicate that one person can cause another to sin. Therefore, it is my opinion that He is pointing the wrong doing at the man that divorces his wife. Jesus clarifies by stating "for fornication". It is wrong to divorce someone simply to have sex with someone else. Jesus is saying when there is a marriage agreement in place, we are hurting our partner (our neighbor) if we divorce for the sake of lust.

Again, if I was the head of a religious group and it was part of my agenda to discourage divorce, I could quote biblical opinion. But I could not say that God said in the commandments not to divorce. Ultimately, what Jesus teaches us is to treat one another as we would like to be treated. Therefore, when two people are joined in marriage they should respect and treat one another in accordance with the agreement they entered, but divorce is not a sin.

Additionally, Jesus warns us not to judge. I must admit, prior to my divorce, I was what I would call a divorce snob. I thought that people who divorced were quitters and that under circumstances that don't involve abuse, couples should stay married. I guess it took two divorces to curve my judgmental and superior attitude. God wants us to live according to His commandments and be joyful and fulfilled in life. If He were against divorce, He would have most certainly indicated so within the commandments as He did of adultery.

I have never believed that my God wanted me to stay in a marriage that was horrible. When my husband and I divorced, I am positive from the peace in my heart that it was the right decision. I am the happiest single woman alive. I thank God every day for the strength to make it through the divorce and the happiness that it has given me. I am living proof that God abundantly blesses us regardless of our past…whatever it may be.

HOMOSEXUALITY

There are many controversial topics politicians love to discuss or live to avoid, depending of course on the popularity of their stance on the subject at hand. Everyone knows that in order to get elected, it is critical to voice the most popular response rather than the individual's honest opinion. This is an unfortunate reality because the signals are so mixed. I'm certain our children, without good parental guidance, are very confused about what is morally correct.

One of the hot topics of debate is homosexuality. Specifically, if it is acceptable for two members of the same sex to legally marry. I am thankful today that I am not a politician and that I have the platform and freedom to speak openly.

The seven last commandments are all designed so that we love and honor ourselves and more importantly, others. I believe that because God and Jesus did not touch upon the subject of homosexuality in any way, it cannot be sinful. Further, I believe the evil lies in judging our neighbors. But just because I do not believe it is a sin and perhaps you do, the key is to remain neutral where there is clearly no concise answer.

I do not have any friends or family members who are gay. Not by choice, I just simply don't know any. But I know from the feeling of peace I receive when pondering right from wrong.

I once worked at a coffee house in my teens in which I had a coworker who was admittedly gay. He was a really nice guy from a wonderful family. One day I gave him a ride home from work and went inside to meet his mom.

As I walked around their family room looking at all of their pictures I noticed a family portrait in which he and his siblings were very young. Dan looked as though he was about five years old. His brothers looked athletic and confident. Dan was smiling in the picture from ear to ear looking as happy as a child could be. He stood next to me and said "I even knew it then". I remember thinking "wow, this was never a choice for him".

After getting to know him, one day he relayed the painful story of how he had battled his feelings for years and had tried so many times to be attracted to girls. He told me about the day that he broke the news to his parents; stating he felt practically suicidal that day. He said that his mom accepted immediately and his dad came around within a short period of time.

I've not seen him in twenty years but I am thankful for the privilege to know him because it is easy to ascertain my stance. There is no reason in the world for a seventeen year old boy to put himself through the agony and pain of having to stand in front of his parents and make that announcement. It pains me to think of the suffering he and anyone else has had to endure because we, an agenda based society, judged and said it was wrong. If two women are living together in matrimony with blissful happiness; how does that hurt anyone else?

The Bible DOES NOT have a commandment against homosexuality. In fact, the person, people, church, or pastor that quotes Leviticus 20 as stating that The Bible condemns a man lying with mankind is wrong. These people do not, *in my opinion*, have a fair understanding of scripture.

Leviticus takes verse after verse clearly outlining what relatives we cannot have sexual relations with. It continues by prohibiting sex with a beast or animal. It then states man may not lie with "mankind" as he lies with a woman, or they are *both* in sin. Now, I may not have majored in

English but I am fairly sure one would not use the term "both" when referencing mankind. At this point, we must ask the question, why was the word "mankind" used as opposed to the word "man"? Shouldn't the verse read "man shall not lie with a man as he does with a woman"? Isn't the entire point to warn against man having intercourse with another man? Or is it ok for man to have intercourse with another man just not with several men, hence the use of the word "mankind"? In this King James Version, the use of the word "mankind" and the word "both" indicates that the rule's clarity was lost in translation, because it doesn't make sense. It could be a rule against homosexuality or it could be a rule against a man and woman engaging in orgies; with this use of "both" and "mankind". But common sense tells us that if so many words were used within Leviticus to prohibit man and sister-in-law, man and daughter-in-law etc., the words would have additionally been used to clarify man with *another* man. Additionally, words would have been used to prohibit woman with another woman! This is key because in this particular book, it is all gender specific utilizing man with sister and woman with beast and so on. So with this long list of rules regarding who one cannot engage with sexually, why is there no sister and sister-in-law, or man with his brother, or woman with her mother, and an entire list of that nature?

I find this another classic example of someone interpreting the Bible with his own agenda against homosexuality. These vague references to homosexuality in Leviticus and Romans are ambiguous at best. Therefore, unless Jesus said it or God ordained it within The Ten Commandments, we can no longer trust one man's interpretation that snowballed into today's mass interpretation that homosexuality is in the Bible. The bottom line is if God specifically requires us to love our neighbors but never specifically ruled on homosexuality, do we really want to risk our inheritance on a possible misinterpretation? We must make a stand today to stamp out the horrible treatment we have given. If we do not, we are choosing to defy God in three huge aspects.

- ✓ Failure to love our neighbor
- ✓ Judging and hatred
- ✓ Following another's discernment
- ✓ Adding to God's laws

Again to emphasize, there is nothing wrong with unconventional sexual preferences because they do not HURT anyone. There is EVERYTHING wrong with not equally loving every person on Earth.

PROMISCUITY, PRE-MARITAL SEX, MASTURBATION, AND UNCONVENTIONAL SEX

What about indiscriminate sex? Or having sex every day with a different partner each time? Or marrying more than one person? In the Old Testament, Jacob married two sisters and had children with the maid. If I were a religious leader that wanted to encourage polygamy I could simply reference this historical event as God's approval of this practice. But the truth is, God tells us not to commit adultery. God wants us to have one partner at a time and requires that we are faithful to that partner. That is why there is a commandment dedicated to having one partner.

Masturbation often begins in the teenage years simultaneously with the guilt of the act itself. I feel huge sympathy for the teenage boy that is made to feel guilty for an action that hurts no one. It is not a sin to masturbate or it would be in scripture. God never concerned himself with these petty rules. If I had to take a stab at whether or not God would want a man or woman to be sexually frustrated or satisfied, my money would be on satisfied because God doesn't like His children to suffer. It is not in the commandments.

There are a surprising amount of adults that I have found feeling they cannot serve and be loyal to God because of their sexual preferences.

I recently read a book by which two consenting responsible adults engaged in, let's just say it, kinky sex. He introduces her to his entire repertoire of spanking, blindfolding, bounding, and sexual toys. Although a very innocent girl, he never takes one step without her sincere permission. She falls in love with both the man and the extreme sexual gratification she receives from his apparent expertise.

My friend gave me the book and insisted I read it. She was curious as to my opinion of whether the book and the main character crossed the line in sin engaged in the "kinkery" he enjoyed with sex.

There is no sin here. The Bible and commandments don't forbid pleasure in sex, just the monogamy of it; and these two characters were. Remembering that we must never hurt anyone else, what happens between two consenting adults is not in any way a sin. It is ridiculous to believe that God would frown upon it.

What God would frown upon is an otherwise good person who is not living in faith because he or she likes to have fun with their partner. Additionally, there is nothing sexier than a fun loving person who lives in faith!

Stop limiting yourself because of age old agendas; it is not only acceptable but encouraged to live life to the fullest.

CHAPTER 5} LOVING EVERYONE

It seems an easy request. I used to think that it is something I don't even need to work on; I'd give the shirt off my back to a stranger. At one time I served on five different church committees and volunteered everywhere from meals in need to the bereavement ministry. I was convinced that loving came natural to me.

But I, like many, found it easy to love most of my family, my friends, my children and even strangers, but that is not what God meant. It is easy to love those that love us. It is easy to give a stranger a twenty dollar bill and believe we love him. But Jesus explains to us that it is our enemies that we must learn to love.

When we complete this difficult task, it renders every person in our life powerless. When we can no longer be hurt by man because we love our enemies, we are free. It is now balanced to the center of the scale in the perfect stability of oneness with God.

Because we are on the journey to the perfectness that God intended, praying for our enemies is only half of the battle. It is when we truly want our enemy to be a reinholder and then a rainmaker that the war is won. It is one thing to pray for their soul but quite another to WANT our enemy to achieve greatness and receive His promise. That's tough! But when we receive that transformation, we have officially joined the army of angels that's true mission is for oneness with humanity and God.

God tells us to love everyone with no exceptions. He doesn't want us to love everyone but our ex-spouse or everyone but the people who have severely wronged us. It turns out that the quality that I thought I **had** most was the quality I **lacked** MOST. It came natural to me to love everyone except a select few. I told myself I loved my enemies because I was always kind to them. But that is not enough.

Unfortunately, I had to go through a very painful experience for God to show me the error of my ways…

As We Love Ourselves

I was evicted from my home and the landlord was vicious. I was several months late and certainly she had just cause. We went to court and I pleaded with her to allow us to stay; I put in writing that I would not only pay the arrears but four months of advance rent to make up for the delinquency. She said because that was three weeks away, she didn't trust that I would receive my commission, even though I had proof of funds from my company. My attorney suggested that because I owned my car free and clear, that perhaps I could sign it over to her for the three week interim. She agreed.

When I got home, I could not find the title to the car. I frantically called my attorney and he said he would call hers and see if I applied for a lost title she would accept a legal lien against the car. She agreed to the paperwork.

The next morning at nine a.m. the sheriff knocked on our door and informed me we were being evicted. I kindly informed him that we had gone to court yesterday and an agreement was reached verbally; our attorneys were writing the addendum as we speak. The sheriff looked at me in judgmental doubt as if to say "sure lady". I went on to explain that the landlord must have forgotten to call him. He then informed me that the landlord and her husband were in the car parked by the curb and this was, in fact, under her authority.

I quickly called my attorney and he indicated that because we'd agreed in court, that this was just a mistake and he would handle it. He called me several minutes later and said he had never seen anything like this person in all of his years of practice. He said she was completely unreasonable, and that she would lose thousands of dollars in doing this, but she was adamant about the eviction.

I then pleaded with her husband. I explained that because my commission wasn't arriving for three weeks, I was penniless and there was nowhere for the kids and I to go. I told him I would bring him cash in one hour. He asked his wife and she said no. I told him that I would borrow as much cash as they needed to allow me to stay. I said my kids adored the house and all of their friends were there and that they would be devastated. I also told him that if he didn't care about the money, we have no family here therefore no movers or anyone to help us. The couple not only turned down thousands of dollars, they told me to get our personal belongings and leave.

The sheriff informed me that instead of using the sheriff's help for belongings, they opted to do it themselves. They employed two hired hands for the heavy things. Their plan for all of the rest of our items was to move it themselves. They started with trash bags and ended with just throwing our belongings into the garden dirt. In a huge trash pile they threw our family photos, clothes, pillows, toys, books, and dishes.

As I was packing a few suitcases, I could hear her husband breaking my dishes as he packed. I never flinched. I was proud of my spiritual growth because I looked him in the eye and said " I can't possibly understand your decision to turn down cash and turn a woman and five children onto the street but I accept you've made your choice and I will never think unkindly of you or speak poorly about you in the community. With your permission and with your supervision, I will continue to pack and work until you would like me to leave so that you don't have to do so much." He agreed clearly overwhelmed with the amount of our possessions; also puzzled by my lack of negative emotions.

He overheard me telling someone on the phone that I felt great; that in spite of the eviction my faith was strong and that the kids and I would be fine. He, at that point, told the sheriff to escort me off of the premises. He was clearly upset that I felt great. These people wanted me to be in pain; it was their mission. It wasn't about money.

When the kids were released from school that day and I broke the news to them; they were devastated. They couldn't stop crying and they couldn't understand. They kept asking if we could just go inside and sit in the hallway. They wanted to lie on their beds. I could not tell them their mattresses and furniture was lying in the backyard in a heap.

We went to McDonalds and hung for several hours as my parents wired money for food and paid for a hotel.

That evening, after moving my belongings in the freezing darkness of a cold winter night, I was exhausted. I couldn't wait for my head to hit the pillow.

I didn't fall asleep until five a.m. I kept arrogantly patting myself on the back in my thoughts. I had managed to bestow nothing but kindness to the evilness that was my landlord. I remembered the years that I myself had been a landlord. I was so superior to them because I had a similar situation with a single mother who was over six months late, even though I was in dire financial straits; I let her stay and forgave the delinquent months when she retained employment.

I kept thinking about what scripture says about hurting people intentionally, about hurting children, and especially how God punishes people who hurt those of us who live in faith. I felt so superior. I thought, I should have warned the landlord that their lives will be full of strife for their poor choice of actions.

I then had revelation. I realized at that moment that I am far guiltier. I have studied scripture; I know to love my neighbor as myself. I was lying in that hotel bed reveling in the fact that something far worse than an eviction was inevitable for them. I realized I wanted them to feel pain; the girl who thought she loved everyone! I had judged them as evil but I was just as evil. I was kind in my words to them; but I didn't love my neighbors!

I realized that night that if I love them as much as I love me, I would not be having these thoughts. This is what Jesus meant! Jesus was telling us when we can love our enemies TO THE EXTENT that we long for their faith, belief, and happiness to EXCEED ours is the day that we have graduated Love Thy Neighbor 101.

Like The Quakers, I should not only pray that my landlord does not encounter hardships; I should pray that they become one with God. I should pray they reach a level of faith that enables much success and happiness. I should be true to that prayer and have a sincere want of goodness for them in my heart.

It is easy to love those that love us, we must love those that hate us, those who have wronged us and those who share a different belief. That is how we all become one. Jesus came to earth to teach this principle. His mission was to teach us how to live in harmony with others.

WITHOUT JUDGMENT

There was a gentleman on the subway in New York with his four and seven year old sons. He was reading the newspaper and his head was down. His kids were unruly, loud and boisterous. The four year old was loud and making faces. The seven year old was rude and even kicked others and their belongings. The father was ridiculous in his blatant disregard for his children's behavior. He never even lifted his head.

Finally, a woman said to the man "Excuse me, sir, but your son just kicked my shin and I think I can speak for all in saying that your children are disrupting everyone and we are appalled that you've said nothing to them".

The man absently looked at the woman and said, "Ma'am, I'm very sorry. We have just left the hospital. My wife and their mother just died. She was struck by a car right after I met her at the office for lunch. The kids are confused and sad and I am completely numb. I apologize for their behavior. I guess right now we don't know how to act."

Whenever we start to judge, we are making an assumption based on only part of the facts. Most often one thing we witnessed or one story we heard. To judge is wrong and we must take care to remember stories such as the one above and always remain open minded.

Have you ever cursed (even silently) a driver that is going deliberately slow and making you late for work? I know that I have. Sometimes we are so certain and entirely positive that we know all of the facts that we judge unknowingly. The gentleman that is going 35 MPH in a 65 zone could have an issue with his car overheating and he is taking his child that we cannot see in the backseat to the hospital. We just don't know. Let us all make our best effort to live like Jesus and by His example on Earth.

AVOID GOSSIP AND WRONG DOING

Gossip is an evilness that masquerades as harmless socialization or helpful information. When we socialize, there are so many great things to convey. We must remember to always speak of the great things and wonderful accomplishments of others. God has blessed us with a multitude of topics from interesting places to football. "Did you hear about what happened to Joe" should never be uttered unless Joe won the Heisman.

Proverbs 6:20

Where no wood is, there the fire goeth out; so where there is no tale-bearer the strife ceaseth.

One of the most well thought analogies in scripture; this sentence says it all in reference to gossip and spreading innuendos. There is absolutely no good reason to report other's bad news. It is a sign of a deficiency within the tale bearer.

When the landlord cast all of my belongings in the dirt and grass, before I could even call my older children, they were already informed. There was more than one neighbor that instead of asking me if there was anything they could do to help, they asked themselves who do I know that she knows that I can tell this juicy piece of gossip?

God did so much work within me that night. I am sure in my life I have been the gossiper instead of The Samaritan. It is my hope that I never make that mistake again. I hope to always be a help to my neighbor, not a hindrance.

It is not acceptable to tell a story of someone, even if it's true, if it sheds them in a bad light. A person that is simply reporting the facts is causing strife in another's life. We do not love our neighbor if we are talking about him to another. We must ask ourselves am I adding wood onto the fire or am I letting that fire die? Be the person that kills the fire by never repeating gossip. If at all possible, if someone begins to gossip, kindly excuse yourself or say "I'd rather not listen if this is gossip."

I have a friend who works in a very competitive industry with a close knit office. She is married with four children and her salary is crucial to the family's income and well-being. With the present economy, she cannot afford to lose her job.

Her struggle is not to gossip about the people who are gossiping about her. After all, it's only fair right? These people drew first blood and if she doesn't at least partake to defend herself it could be detrimental to her family.

My advice to her was to do her job, do it well, address any concerns only with the person that it is related to, and God will handle the rest. Love and treat each person as you would like them to love and treat you.

Often we justify sinful behavior by necessity. "Look, I am a great person but if I do not report to the boss when I see Cindy sneak in late then our boss is going to think I am the only one late, and Cindy is late more than I am". We believe that there is justification in snitching because we tell ourselves we are just trying to survive, that we have to feed our kids.

But truthfully we know that two wrongs don't make a right. The best course of action is to confront her kindly and in private. Never be ugly, judging, or condescending. "Hey, the boss talked to me about tardiness and I thought maybe it was you that told her, I noticed that you were a little late today. Could we make a pact to stick together and not report the little things, I am really working on getting to work on time".

Most people are reasonable. Some people are confrontational and cannot be reasoned with but most importantly, we must know that we handled the situation with love, and that we sincerely want this person to receive all that God has to offer.

Vengeance and hatred cannot be present simultaneously in our heart with pure love of all. Vengeance is mine says Our Lord because of His love for us. Scripture says that

God will heap coals upon the heads of our enemies. Western civilization likes to boast "I don't believe in karma", but the truth is, scripture promises its premise. If we judge, we will be judged and if we measure, we will be measured etc. We don't have to use the term "karma", but inevitably we will reap what we sow.

Because vengeance is such a dangerous action, God makes His intentions clear in saying to the faithful; don't worry, I will take care of it. This is His way of protecting our heart from evil. Our job is to love and want our enemy to have faith in God, once we achieve this level of pureness, our job is done. Leave the rest to Him.

SEPARATION OF CHURCH AND CHURCH

Choosing the correct rules is a difficult task, but choosing rules we must now refrain from is sometimes harder.

There was a time as a Catholic that I felt sorry for other denominations. Especially Islamic and Jewish; just certain the followers were so far from the truth.

The Muslim faith gave me discomfort knowing how our beliefs are polar opposite. As I read my first book on this faith, I was fascinated and amazed at the similarities between their beliefs and mine. I was simply amazed that they too believe in one God. I was stunned that they believe and accept Noah, Moses, Abraham, Jacob, and yes... even Jesus. They believe, like the Jewish faith, that Jesus was a great prophet and not divine. But their belief in prayer, and angels, and being rewarded for good deeds on earth are the same as mine. I can't express the amount of pleasure I felt knowing we have the same basic belief system.

I felt embarrassed at my ignorance. I believe in one God, I believe in Jesus Christ his only son, and I believe that it is an honor to be His daughter and to serve Him. I finally feel closeness with all denominations based on our One Glorious God. We are all one.

I also believe that I do not have all the answers, nor do the Muslims, the Jews or any other denomination. I know this; we are all His children. I recently met a very fascinating woman, I had no idea why I was drawn to her but for some reason, I felt compelled to converse. Her name is Laura and she works on a farm. She began speaking of God because we had found one of the many peacock feathers around the farm. She indicated that the colorful part that looks like an eye is traditionally symbolic of God.

We had a brief discussion about God by which I said "if you have faith, you know your Redeemer lives". She boldly corrected me and said "just because you believe that Jesus is divine as I do, you must not say that those that believe He is **not** do not have faith". I had to tell her that I stand corrected, and I am appreciative to her for the correction. I now take delight in knowing more about the Muslim faith. It is an important lesson to learn, we must never judge any other person or group.

Ponder this. If the Muslim and Christian population are the two largest in the world; with a combined total of over three billion believers, isn't it a fair conclusion that both religions are acceptable to our God? If the Jewish and the Muslims believe in one God but that Jesus existed as a prophet rather than the son of God, and Christians believe in the divinity of Christ; isn't it fair to say that we are all, at the least, one in faith with one God. If the primary difference is the role of Jesus; who is correct? We will only know when the answer is revealed; therefore we must live in unity and coexist as His children.

Each religious group, faith, church and/or denomination is founded by a person or group of people with his/her/their own interpretation of The Bible. The only entity that can answer correctly chose not to enlighten us with the answer. Additionally, He pleads us to love our neighbors, and to never judge them. It is with this divine request that we must take care to not consider ourselves the right church or the right pastor with the right religion; ever.

So which denomination is the one with correct procedure to be with faith? Obviously if this question was posed in a meeting hall with a representative of each; each priest, pastor as well as follower would raise his/her hand. Have any of you that is a member in a church gotten a distress signal, an unsettling feeling in your spirit, when you ponder the correct answer?

The answer is simple. God gave us the answer and Jesus diligently taught us in His time on earth. Jesus said to love thy neighbor as thyself, don't judge him, don't speak poorly of him, and certainly don't think yourself better than him. Therefore, all of the denominations that love God and choose Him are valid.

There is no correct church. The Bible doesn't instruct specific prophets to build a church and designate rules and regulations to follow based on his interpretation of the rules found in The Bible. The Bible does not further instruct this pastor or priest to only choose the rules found that **he** feels are relevant to true faith in God. In fact, the last chapter of Revelations warns man the terrible fate of the person that dares to add or delete rules to live by in faith.

There are many wonderful churches in the world and if the church gives inspiration and knowledge to assist on the path to faith in God, by all means, one should attend. In my limited study of specific denominations, the Quakers seem the most bible based and commandment oriented religion that I have studied. The responsibility in choosing a church is to ask oneself two relevant questions. Is the church I attend bible-based and focused on the word of God? And secondly, does the church require its members to follow rules that are **not** part of The Ten Commandments?

Jesus is very adamant, almost to the point of begging in His love for us, to only follow the commandments and rules set by God. It is because He is one with God that He does this. His words are not minced when He instructs us to only partake in the commandments and what His Father designates. If we decided to use every written rule in The Bible, with man's interpretation of how it should be followed, and *which* rules to follow, one couldn't begin to imagine what that faith would look like. We would be dragging livestock to church for offering as well as some other farfetched rituals...

- When a farmer forgets some stalks of harvest, he may not retrieve them, he must leave them for strangers
- If your brother owes you money, you may not go into his house to collect, rather you must stay outside and let someone bring it to you
- When a man takes a wife, he may not go to war or go to work, but stay home to "cheer up" his wife for one year following the nuptials
- No garments may be worn of a wool and linen blend

Of course these are silly interpretations of the laws written in Deuteronomy. Someone thousands of years ago wrote these laws according to the times; with his own ideology, clearly. The important and critical thing to remember is that when the Old Testament was written, it was a hand book for living. Many of the "rules" were implemented for safe living in the times. Women are instructed the correct procedure for handling menstruation hygiene. Our God did not create laws regarding the proper procedure for handling menstruation. Can you imagine our God considering it sinful to not follow the menstruation guidelines?

Man has taken parts of the handbook portion of The Old Testament and used some of the rules of the times for his/her own agenda. We know the rules that we are supposed to follow in the Bible are the rules pertaining to His commandments. Period.

Now, this may make some people uncomfortable. But the fact is there is a huge responsibility when we understand what God wants from us. Therefore, if your church requires you to follow a rule or ritual that does not give you peace, you must refrain from it.

I never felt peace going to confession in the Catholic church. It made my peace compass spin out of control. As I would stand outside the confessional awaiting my turn, my palms would sweat; knowing I soon had to confess that I was the serial killer in the community that the authorities had been searching for. I had to remind myself that I had never killed anyone; that I had only told a lie or two and had not gone to church. But I felt like the serial killer! The feeling of anxiety didn't come from my sin, it came from my logic. I knew in my heart that when we repent of our sins it is between ourselves and God. It never felt natural to me. If you are Catholic, do not take my advice regarding confession, read scripture and decide for yourself.

Ignorance is bliss in this regard. If you have practiced a certain ritual all of your life that was taught to you in your church as a child, and you **now** feel it is not pleasing to God, He will forgive you for sin in ignorance of course. But with the gained knowledge through your walk in faith that it is wrong; you must refrain from continuing the practice. Always practice as you feel you have learned for yourself is the true way to practice, and never allow any other entity to change that.

It is critical for us to know that God is all knowing and therefore has given us precisely the amount of knowledge we are supposed to have. Therefore, all religious denominations are accurate if they serve one God, we may not judge he who calls whom we call God, another name. It is also imperative that we do not judge another's faith by his practice. No one person or church knows who is correct. God gave us the perfect amount of knowledge to live with faith in Him. We must be careful and diligent in loving everyone; as Jesus asks of us through The Father.

Jesus was telling us in the easiest terms, in the easiest way with the story of the good Samaritan. He instructs to help and love people that aren't your first pick to help or even your one hundredth. It's easy to help nurse your mom back to health, even a stranger in a nursing home that reminds you of your grandmother. But what about the homeless man from Jamaica with no teeth that smells of liquor? What about the Jewish family that lost their income that you have always disliked? What about the girl you attend school with that has no one to sit with in the cafeteria? If you are the most popular girl in school, are you popular in the eyes of God if you do not invite her to sit with you as your peer? Ask her to sit with you and your friends, you will be so happy you did. Giving of your company alone is pleasing to God.

LOVE your neighbor the Muslim, your neighbor the Christian, your neighbor the geek, your neighbor the drug addict; and never judge. Who is to say who is correct? You know Who.

Karen 2013   Kara and Karen 2011 NY

Kaitie and Karen Homecoming 2011

Noah, Kent, and Julia Dauphin Island 2010

The whole crew: Julia, Kaitie, Kent, Noah, Kara, and Karen 2012

CHAPTER 6} LOVING YOU FOR YOU

God gave us the looks, personality, talents, faults, assets and liabilities for the dream in our heart. There is not one element of our design that was unintentional. There will be a day that we will understand. It is extremely important to be thankful for what we were given remembering that His dream for us is huge. If we are truly thankful of our own flaws we are much more understanding to the flaws of others.

There is a huge transformation that occurs with faith both on the inside as well as our outward appearance. Once we begin to truly love ourselves as well as those around us, our entire demeanor and attitude is barely recognizable to the people that have known us our entire lives. Because this change is divine, it is a little difficult for us to perceive much less our family and friends. We can attempt to change one thousand times with no success. It is only when we start making changes AND making a relationship with God that the change is apparent, irreversible, and effective. Only God can help with this type of transformation. That is why the other nine hundred ninety nine attempts were unsuccessful. Thank God for the awesome traits you do have.

Divine Transformation- a complete and successful change under the authority, supervision, and assistance of God which could not be accomplished in the natural way of man.

In order to change our thinking, our compassion level, our sympathy, personality, humility, and feelings we must first build an honest relationship with God. He will not invest in this magnitude of conversion with a stranger.

The advantage of divine transformation is that with His help, the insecurities we used to harbor about our looks or deficiencies will evaporate as we focus on the gift of happy living.

There is also another part of self-love that is difficult to understand but must be conquered. In the most basic terms, it is when we take the part of our personality that is one way and join it to the portion of our personality that is opposite.

Jesus makes many references to the concept that when two or more are gathered in his name, God will be there. But in The Gospel of Thomas, it is worded like this:

The Gospel of Thomas:

"When you make the two one, you will become the sons of man and when you say mountain, move away, it will move away".

Also:

"If two make peace with each other in this one house, they will say to the mountain move away and it will move away."

It is compelling when Jesus gives this advice, He uses the figure one, two and three (in another version) rather than many or hundreds or thousands. It would stand to reason that if two in agreement can move a mountain, then a congregation could change the world. But Jesus taught with parables. It could be that the numbers two and three becoming one simply means when our spirit is in direct line with our mind and our personality joins our intellect with the belief. It is at this point that we have officially become one with God and the power to move mountains is imminent.

Like the story of the prodigal son, speaking in a parabolic sense, one son is responsible and hardworking while the other is frivolous and irresponsible. It is only through the father that the reconciliation occurs. This is symbolic of us. Just when we are sure that we completely believe, one little thing goes wrong and our brain says "see I told you this reinholder/ rainmaker thing is bullshit, I just got a speeding ticket". Instead, we must embrace the one personality and handle bumps in the road with grace, peace, and the understanding that the speeding ticket and other life happenings cannot define or diminish our oneness with Him.

When we hear that we can easily obtain all that God has to offer there is a part of our personality that disbelieves, tries to create doubt and nags at the believing part of our personality saying "you don't deserve it, who do you think you are, only hard work will get you anywhere", on and on until our brain is in a never ending battle to decipher the truth. The truth is that the speeding ticket did not happen by chance. Reinholders get speeding tickets all the time, the question is; are you going to drop the reins over a stupid ticket?

It is only when we join our intellect to our belief system that the oneness with God truly occurs. Stay the course. Stand strong, and keep pushing forward as a child of God and your life will forever change from what you once knew. Greatness is coming.

But there is also another aspect of joining two intricate parts of faith together and it deals with our thoughts and actions. This is a critical entity of self-love.

Imagine yourself shipwrecked on an unchartered island alone. The island is abundant with fruits and vegetables, trees for shade and plenty of fish and even lobster that may easily be caught. Even though everything that you technically need to survive is abundant on this island, your heart longs for the comforts of home, your family, and all of your friends back home.

A plan would, of course, have to be enacted to either be rescued or get off of the island. The plan would probably be a three part design.

- ✓ Build a shelter to stay in the interim
- ✓ Create and erect a large visible distress sign
- ✓ Make a sea-worthy catamaran or boat to escape the island and search for civilization

This three part plan has many smaller steps to achieve the ultimate goal to save you and get home; the designing and building of a boat would be a multi-faceted plan in it of itself. I imagine if it were me, by the time I had created shelter and a distress signal, I would procrastinate the huge task of the boat plan. I can see myself full of the doubt of both my ability as well as the probability of success. As a woman, it may seem silly but I've always thought I can build anything if I put my mind to it. I've built shelves and simple tables and repaired things around the house. I get the job done but not always in the fastest and most aesthetically pleasing way. The boat would be a difficult task but having faith that it would weather the sea and bring me to civilization would take mammoth faith indeed.

Phases	Steps	Like
Phase One	Design a blueprint	Scripture
Phase Two	Create material list	Seek
Phase Three	Collect raw materials	Wisdom
Phase Four	Construct hardware	Thoughts
Phase Five	Build hull	Actions
Phase Six	Build sails and rudder	Direction
Phase Seven	Assemble all parts	Live in faith

Getting back to civilization from being shipwrecked is a great analogy of the work involved for The Rainmaker. It may seem a huge task, but sooner or later it has to be done. Just as we could live out eternity on the island, we can also live in this type of mediocrity called life. Every day we wait to build the boat just prolongs our great destiny. Once built, if we do not have the faith to set sail unto the violent seas, we cannot possibly reach the vast goodliness of an extraordinary life. When the seas are rough, we must believe and never doubt; always following the rules to the best of our ability.

Unfortunately, once we have assembled the boat is when the uncertain journey begins. Reaching our divine destiny is contingent on how we maneuver each wave. It may seem a cheesy comparison, but truer words were never spoken; some of the waves will be small and last for days, and sometimes it may be one huge wave that nearly breaks your boat to pieces. The key is how we handle both the small and massive waves.

While on the journey, it is **imperative** that we:

- Treat our children nicely when we find ourselves suddenly unemployed
- Love our enemy that has turned the entire town against us with their lies by wanting more for him than for ourselves
- Choose to be honest in business in every way and follow God's laws
- Never gossip or revel in someone's misfortune by "telling the tale"
- Love and speak to God always and often; even through the huge waves
- Stay faithful, when the easy way is to cheat
- Leave vengeance to God knowing that passing on evil is the ultimate ticket to power

But most importantly, it is impossible to hold the power of the rainmaker if one facet is missing; just as it is impossible to set sail without a rudder or hull. We may attempt to brave the open sea, but deep within us we know that we did not build that hull to be sea-worthy or rushed the making of the sail.

We must examine not only our actions, but our heart daily. One of the most gratifying essentials of self-love is knowing that our heart is in line with Our Father. I can give countless examples of when I was **doing** the right thing, but my thinking was completely mucked.

Recently, I went in on a gift for someone. It was a fairly expensive gift but something this person not only needed, but the gift would give him great joy. It was just too expensive to give on my own, so a family member suggested we split it 50/50. When I went to pick up the gift, this person said he would pay me on the day we gave it. On the day we gave the gift, he said he would pay me next week, that he would have it then. Needless to say, it was never mentioned again. I am positive this is why scripture instructs us to give as oppose to lend. No inner struggles can evolve from giving.

For quite a while, every time I saw this individual, I would consider asking him for the money. I was proud of myself for never mentioning it. But was I really maintaining what God asks of me?

Matthew 12:25And Jesus knew their thoughts, and said unto, Every kingdom divided against itself is brought to desolation, and every

> *city or house divided against itself*
> *shall not stand.*

This is a vastly telling parable regarding our thoughts. Jesus spoke in every day allegories that could understandably relate for many generations. Cities and houses and kingdoms are entities we can understand, but He is clearly giving this analogy about the topic of our thoughts. He is indicating very concisely that a person whose heart is divided against his actions cannot obtain or maintain the self-love emitted from the firm foundation of thoughts and actions joined harmoniously. Further, he gives the consequence for the failure as desolation and an unfit foundation.

This is why scripture emphasizes to refrain from sinning in our heart; not because God will be offended but because God knows the very essence of loving ourselves begins with clearing our mind of this negativity.

As for my personal situation, as soon as I changed my thought pattern to the fact that this person no longer owed me the money; that it was gifted and not loaned, is the moment I had eternal peace on the matter. Now I no longer loan money; I simply give what I can, sometimes I even give more than what is asked, never expecting repayment. This feels great all the way around, creating the self-love that God wants for us.

Proverbs 16:3

Commit thy works unto the Lord, and thy thoughts shall be established.

When we just do good and give for the sake of giving, our thoughts will soon move over to more goodness. Good deeds lead the mind to good thoughts.

Chapter 7} Giving Alms & Doing Works

There was a profound lesson in works that came from that night of eviction. As I called my little girl's friend's parents to ask if the kids could come over while I packed, her dad asked what I was going to do. He suggested I rent a large truck. I said I would if I could afford it but I was limited and therefore would just do the best I could in the late hour. I was going to simply move my things that I could into the storage that my parents paid for. I couldn't afford to rent a truck. The sheriff said my furniture would be discarded in the morning if not retrieved from the backyard. Since my oldest daughter was working, I knew of no one to even help.

The girl's dad, Jim, hung up with me and called back roughly ten minutes later stating I should bring the kids over because he had made spaghetti and meatballs and his teenage son would watch the kids. He very casually said "I rented a twenty six foot moving truck for you but I am in a bit of a hurry because the rental store closes in less than an hour. Oh, and I called my cousin and he will help **me** move the big furniture." He didn't say "us", he said "me". He had already made a definitive plan as to how to get all of my possessions. This was a man I'd met one time in passing!

Another dad whose daughter plays with my kids grabbed his teenage son and helped for the duration. My daughter and her boyfriend showed up with a huge trailer in tow. Jim's wife pulled up to pitch in after working a 12 hour day. It was dark and freezing, I couldn't feel my toes after twenty minutes, but no one complained. I cannot remember a colder day in the history of St. Louis.

Seven Samaritans worked until every huge and heavy furniture piece was stowed and each belonging was rescued from the dirt and grass.

To this day, I cannot even think of the selflessness and kindness of these people without welling with tears. Most people dread helping their friends and family move. God sent seven angels to help me when I had no one.

I can only hope that in my lifetime I can make a difference like that. In Matthew it says when you help, not to brag about it later. These people wanted nothing in return; only to help. It was Jim's only day off. My daughter, Kaitie, had an early flight to catch. Her boyfriend, Travis, had

school early in the morning. Adam, Jim's cousin, had never seen me before in his life; was called to help a stranger move. Jeff, the neighbor, texted me to see if my daughter could play with his and selflessly offered help. Tim, his son, what an exemplary example of a great teenager, sifting through the items as he loaded to be sure there was nothing the kids would mind in storage. Heather, Jim's wife, pulled up at nine p.m. after working a long day and just started systematically grabbing boxes and bags until the last item was on the truck. I wondered if I had worked until nine would I help a stranger move in the bitter cold or choose to go home, put on pjs and watch a movie on my comfy sofa. What a great example of how to live. I vowed that night to be a selfless helper to anyone in need. That is how we are to love others.

Genesis 24/9:

And when she had done giving him drink, she said, I will draw water for thy camels also, until they have done drinking.

I love this story in Genesis, how Rebekah watered all of the camels, walking the many steps to water each one. The water was heavy and it was a lot of work. He asked for a drink, and she gave selflessly of all of her time.

Scripture tells us to give ten percent of what we earn and to always give our "first fruits". We should tithe first before any indulgence. So many people report that the moment they implement tithing, a financial blessing will immediately occur such as the big account they've been working on or a bonus or a pay raise.

Often times tithing is misinterpreted as "giving to the church". If you are positive your church is a worthy asset to your family and the community, you should by all means support that worthy entity. But remember, ten percent truly means to all charitable and reputable causes. Your ten percent can be divided between your church, a homeless family, a person in need, or a charitable organization. The most useful way to ascertain where you need to give is meditating with God; He will guide you to His children in need. Pray with Him about the amount as well, certainly the ten percent rule is a simple minimum.

Another stern warning from Jesus in Matthew is to "not let your left hand know what your right hand is doing". I'll admit I was not the brightest interpreter of biblical phrase. Always above average in English and Literature, I prided myself on the ability to "read between the lines" and grasp underlying meanings. I don't know why this escaped me in religion class, but I just never knew what the heck that expression meant. Reading it as an adult, it's easier to discern and very significant.

Jesus tells us NEVER help someone for the sake of self-indulgence. If you are being charitable because you have a sincere desire to help AND you have prayed and discussed your intention, this is wonderful. But if it is your intention to brag about it later, or just happen to mention it, you have soured the deal. God doesn't like a bragger and neither does man. Never boast about the amount you tithe.

Even if you are helping for all the right reasons, if you talk about it with anyone, it loses favor. He tells us to be so secretive about giving and helping that even one of your hands doesn't know that the other hand helped. How profound is that? Please understand it is conventional to feel happy inside when you've helped...but that happiness will deplete when you talk about it.

Put it to the test. Completely and anonymously help a person, entity, organization, church, or family that you are sure needs it. Ask God for guidance as to whom or what organization is in need. He will give you peace for the right choice. Do it and tell no one, see how it feels. Give to your church, if it is a good church and you feel peace about it, give more than you ever have, tell no one. If you have limited funds, give of your time; such as helping a senior citizen with her yard or babysitting for a mom that needs a moment to herself. If you have not time or money, ask yourself what you have that could be donated.

What Are We Without Works

James 2:15-18

If a brother or sister be naked, and destitute of daily food,

And one of you say unto them, depart in peace, be ye warmed and filled; notwithstanding ye give them not those things which are needful to the body, what doth it profit?

Yea, a man may say, thou hast faith and I have works: shew me thy faith without thy works, and I will shew my faith by my works.

James fills the second chapter of his gospel with the importance of works; doing charitable deeds for those in need. The verse above is in reference to praying for those that are poor, sick, hungry, or in need. He is basically stating that if we are praying for someone to receive food and warmth but we are not helping in that endeavor, we are just a clanging bell. We are just making noise.

If we truly meant our prayer, we would do everything in our power to help.

Further, if we are truly faithful…loving God, ourselves and our neighbor, this is **reflected** by our works. James states that if we have every facet of faith, but have not works, we are not in faith.

We must never simply pray for the homeless woman holding a cardboard sign; we must give her more than we think we should. Have you ever passed a "beggar" with a cup outstretched and gave nothing? I have and still feel terrible about it. I used to work in the city and I told a co-worker one day "I'm not giving money to that guy, he is just a crack addict pretending to be homeless, and I've seen his house". She said something I will never forget. She said "what if he is not and his baby is starving for milk and food, who are you to judge?"

That floored me; even if he is a crack addict, he could die from withdrawals; maybe my money would help him hang on another day until he receives help. Most importantly, if God pulled at your heart to give, trust that feeling and give as generously as you can.

You don't have to take the homeless woman into your home but if you have enough to give her for a hotel, give with all of your heart and what you can afford.

CHAPTER 8} THE MISSING FACET OF THE REINHOLDER

This is an excerpt from my journal not too terribly long ago verbatim (pardon the grammar):

Today I am truly broke. No money. Can't pay the electric bill. Last night I went to the kid's game and it was two dollars to get in. I had 1.95 so they let me in anyway. Because I know God will provide I am fine. But I'm not the best with money so it's kind of funny I bought grocery gift cards and paid the utility bills with the last bit of money I had. It has now been a month and the gift cards are gone. It has been three months since I could buy a cup of coffee, fill my prescriptions, fill my gas tank, take the kids anywhere fun, go to a restaurant, buy the kids clothes, take them through a drive thru, pay my car and health insurance, get my nails done, or go home to see my family.

I thought doing an uncontested divorce with no child support was the right thing to do because we both lost our jobs but he seems to have plenty of money!

I am positive I will thrive soon. I am positive God will give me everything I need. I am so happy today I can't stop smiling, hey I got into the game, and I have food at home. Not the soft pretzel with cheese everybody keeps walking by with but hey someday!

As I just typed that portion of my journal to share with you, I wept. I cried happy tears because I was happy then but happier now. God seasoned me for beauty. He gave me a gift larger than any present a royal family member could purchase. He seasoned me to sweetness! I walked through that desert so that every facet in my life could be sweeter. Not just finances; but the two marriages, the debt, the illnesses, the headaches, the messy house, the terrible unfulfilling job, the heartaches. They were gifts…had I never been through them, THERE IS NO POSSIBLE WAY I would be seasoned to receive like this! A soft pretzel with cheese will never be taken for granted.

Most importantly, I look back on that time in my life and realize a critical element. Every part of my life had changed for the better with one exception; my finances. Looking back, there was one facet of the promise God made to me (abundance) that was missing. Ironically, there was one facet of His rules that I was not following.

Is there one or two facets of faith keeping you from all that God has in store for you?

Joshua is given the message by God with an almighty plan to bring down the walls of Jericho and thus gain access to this wonderful place. The plan was to walk the perimeter of the city once a day and on the seventh day to walk around it seven times. In addition, on the seventh day he was instructed to sound horns and then the walls would come down.

Can you imagine how much faith Joshua had and how much belief he had to possess? It was a crazy and silly plan! It involved literally no actions that would actually remove the wall! If anything, it was ridiculous because the sound of the horns would alert the very people he wanted to defeat. The plan seemed insane. But ultimately, Joshua followed God's instructions to a tee and through belief and faith, the walls were removed. If we believe in The Power of God by living within His laws the laws of power will manifest within us.

I've heard more than one person say "if God truly loved me, He would give me a baby". The truth is, we are all God's children and He loves all of us. If it were as easy as simply asking for a baby, there would be no need of faith. Everyone would have the precise amount of children they would like. Just like our earthly parents, God rewards the children who follow the rules.

If two parents had four children and, because they loved them, rewarded all of the children with anything they wanted, every time they asked, regardless of whether or not they followed the rules; the household would fall into chaos. Eventually, the children would be sick from candy, spoiled from riches, and never have the desire to aspire to be anything more. Sadly, after having pizza, lobster, and ice cream every day for a year, these items would no longer hold the excitement they did before.

But if the parents loved all four children, but only rewarded the ones who followed the rules, it would soon become abundantly clear **how** to receive the parents favor. And more importantly; pizza, lobster, and ice cream would hold value. The parents are setting the rules **more** for the child than for themselves, knowing the children will be happier for it.

God set the rules of faith more for us than for him; knowing that life will be sweeter when we are rewarded with His goodness.

Unfortunately, I believe this is why we receive the tests of life. All humans live by example, when we see someone barren, unable to have a child, and they begin to live in faith and conceive; we believe. We have seen this woman try every medical measure known to man and they have all failed, but when she starts holding the reins and makes her own rain; **we believe.**

When we see someone like me without a college degree who has lost her home and all of her money, and she becomes wealthy; **we believe.**

When we see someone given three weeks to live with terminal cancer and doctors send her home to die, but she begins to walk in faith and believes for healing, then lives 25 more years; then **we believe.**

Just like the parents with four children who only reward the children that follow the rules, God rewards only those who live in faith. By example, others will start to follow.

Stand strong. Don't rely on just doctors for that baby; choose God. Don't just rely on a loan or a lottery ticket to cure debt; choose God. Don't rely merely on a singles group to find the right person; choose God. Live in faith and have it all.

Look at the diagram of the dream and make sure daily that you are walking in faith; doing **all** of the facets, not just **all but one.**

CHAPTER 9} THE FINAL TEST OF THE REINHOLDER

It is said there is always calm before the storm. This, most people find, is especially true of the journey to faith. We begin to walk the journey, we feel like a new person with such delightful calmness about us; then often a storm hits and we question if all of the work we did was in vain. Often times, we'll feel cheated. But the opposite is true; this road block or stumbling block is the sign that we are almost there! The arrival of the storm is the evidence of the power we will soon possess. For me, it was having everything (I had always taken for granted) stripped from me. It seemed like in an instant my job, my home, my bank account and my belongings were gone. I saw my kids on a limited basis and the stress from it all took a physical manifestation; constant sores all over my face. I didn't look good, feel well, and even though material possessions are insignificant; not seeing my children very much nearly killed my spirit.

This storm is the most important time to stay in faith. It has been referred to as the test before the testimony or the mess before the message. Scripturally, it is continually demonstrated within the accounts of David, Jeremiah, Abraham, Isaac, Jacob, Daniel, and many others. It is a prevalent theme that educates us to stay in faith through the storm to receive the ultimate gift on the other side.

Simply stated, when the chips are down; how are we going to treat our children, our co-workers, our spouse, our friends, and the people we don't particularly care for? How will we treat ourselves? How will we treat God? Will we still recognize the commandments, or deviate and call it necessity? Will we discard the hard work and fail this critical test?

Seeking lends to knowledge and knowledge is golden in this regard. Think about it. If you know that your tooth is going to be pulled and it will specifically hurt for about 3 to 5 days, you prepare your mind for the completion of the 5 days and commit to getting the tooth pulled. If the dentist said the pain would be indefinite, most people would not have the surgery. Therefore, these accounts of the storm from David to Daniel are the information we need to stay in faith through the storm. Historically, every person throughout scripture that stayed the course through all setbacks received tremendous and abundant favor.

The Bible says that it is through faith **and patience** that we receive. Therefore, it is critical that we continue to maintain our relationship with God through the storm. It is crucial that we do not snap at our kids, be mean to a co-worker or even worse, cheat on our spouse or steal out of desperation.

I give this account, not to pat myself on the back, but to simply offer by example a situation by which I felt I stayed in faith.

After I lost everything, I took a job in sales for an up and coming company I was hugely excited about. A friend of a friend hired me, he was the founder and creator, and we worked side by side daily to perfect and begin distribution. As we tested the product that he'd been working on for nearly two years, the prototype failed; it didn't work. This was a product directed towards women and I quickly came up with, what I adamantly believed, was the only solution. The gentleman I worked for disagreed and decided to go a different way; what I believed to be very unappealing to women as well as years behind the market. When I pitched my idea to his board, all of the members agreed with me, but he would not budge.

I resigned from the company, not because he did not use my idea, but because after several more months, he could not get the prototype to work. A few days after I quit, two of the members of the board approached me asking me to partner with them to open a company with my idea; the solution I'd come up with and his prototype. I knew that I would make a lot of money and I was completely broke. They even offered to pay me immediately to form the company. This would instantly solve my financial problems, but I also knew that it was wrong. Even though the modification was my idea, his idea was still the basis of the product. It was stealing; the stealing of intellectual property is stealing none the less. I knew it was wrong. The men rationalized by stating "if you were working for a car dealership and decided to open your own, is that wrong?" But cars are cars, this was a never before used product. They then offered, "We all know that he will never get this off of the ground, therefore, why can't we benefit from it?" It was hugely tempting; I knew it would be immensely profitable. But I held fast to my belief system and to this day, I believe I am doing what I love and am successful at it because of the choices I made in the storm to honor the commandments.

Therefore, weather your storm in faith! Stand strong every day knowing that the next day the storm will end. It may take a week and it may take a year but as we learn from scripture, it will end, and it is my belief that it ends sooner for good decisions and a kind disposition. Be kind to your spouse and loving to your children or siblings. When times are fierce and just rough, the tendency to take it out on others gets stronger. Be the person that loves instead of one who snaps, saying "you have no idea what I am going through", nothing justifies meanness. Do your best and apologize when you err.

Chapter 10} The Facets of the Rainmaker

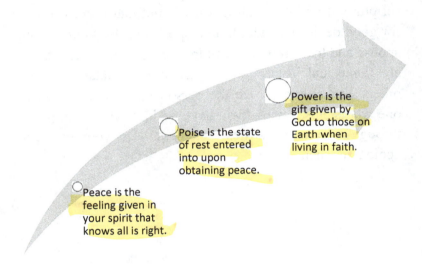

Peace

Many are chosen but few receive is a very disappointing statistic. Many convince themselves that it is too hard. It's devastatingly sad because the irony is that most of us are already following His commandments. Most of us are already a loving and overall good person. How tragic that the only thing standing in the way of all of our dreams coming to fruition is understanding His expectations and fine tuning what we already do. Is the work hard? It is hard. Letting go of a deep seeded grudge against your sister that wronged you or forgiving the man that ruined you financially is difficult. But choosing to hold a grudge verses receiving all that life has to offer is nothing less than absurd.

Peace can only be given by God. It is only through the work of living in faith that the joy of the spirit can bask in peace. It's happiness through The Divine.

POISE

There is a profound beauty of entering the poise and calmness of that which is ultimate faith and belief. When we are positive of the power earned through the accomplishment of faith, love, and belief we are now just simply waiting peacefully in serene anticipation of the excitement of what will now be our life.

But beware. Absence of worry and despair where others believe it should be present causes a confusion to those around you that can only have one explanation; insanity.

Luke 12:53

The father shall be divided against the son, and the son against the father, the mother against the daughter, and the daughter against the mother, the mother in law against the daughter in law, and the daughter in law against the mother in law.

Scripture instructs us through His commandments to honor our mother and father. It is important to God that we do so. But the statement in Luke regarding how we will be divided against a parent is preceded by the division of those who believe and those who do not. Jesus is not referring to those who simply believe in the existence of God, because most of us do.

Jesus plainly clarifies in the next verse when he observes that people who have seen a cloud and know it will rain and feel a wind blow and know it will be followed by heat. They plainly discern the weather by their mind's ability to store the history of statistics of the result of a cloud or a gust of wind. Jesus is perplexed that we cannot store the history of statistics of the result of following God. He is upset that we have read through scripture the result (greatness) of staying in faith throughout difficulties; yet we still doubt.

His stern parable was designed not only as a wakeup call to those who do not believe in the promise, but also as a warning to those that do: don't be surprised if the people who love you most will think you've lost it.

When I realized that I was not going to receive my compensation, my parents were so very worried for me. Each day as my financial situation grew worse, I grew stronger and stronger. I knew two things as I waited in rest; that God was doing necessary work in me and that the more I was tested, the greater the reward. My parents praised my courage. My dad said at one point "your fortitude is exemplary, you inspire me, Karen." They were so supportive; sending me money here and there and offering every bit of moral and financial support they had.

But when things got severely bleak, they said "Karen, you have to get a job." It was ok, it didn't offend me, but there was no way at that point I could explain. I wanted to tell them that I have never been lazy and I am certainly not proud; I would bus tables for 16 hours a day if My Father led me to Ruby Tuesdays. But the fact was, I working double shifts already, writing, it is what I was sure I was supposed to do.

I knew the answer was in writing, but we were divided and there was no point in arguing. If at that point I would have been completely honest, I would've said "when I pray with

God every morning I solemnly request the wisdom and guidance to commit within the day whatever it is He would like me to do, and the only energy I have is to write." Yep; they would've lovingly said "we are driving up there right now".

Don't be surprised when your poise of entering into the rest makes others restless. Don't be discouraged when you cross The Great Divide to unwavering faith and those you thought would join you are divided. As they witness your tests followed by a victory only obtainable by Our Supernatural God, you will by example lead others to begin the walk.

POWER

The power within us...

The power you possess is immeasurable. The power of The Word is within us all. I get tears in my eyes when I think of that very principle. God, just like our earthly parents, not only wants the very best for us, He enabled us the same power to achieve what He Himself has. He empowered us with The Word. With this, the sky is the limit. Any shortcoming we have can be conquered with this power. Any illness, deficit, longing, or pain will be defeated with this principle. Man is the creator of his own heaven just as he creates his own hell.

The Symbol of a Flower

To happen upon a gorgeous flower

Spectacular color of petals and leaves

The thought occurs what was the power

That created the very first to bloom

The joy I feel to know He placed it

With sole intention for me to see

The promise lies within this flower

Of the power that lies inside of me

For every man upon this planet

With ears to hear and eyes to see

Remembers the words that Jesus told us

*The works that I do, he shall do, the **he** that believeth onto Me*

-Karen Delchamps 2011

The curse and the blessing are the same. Bad thoughts on any level must be put away forever. Negativity brings bad things. If we set our minds so that any time we have an evil thought or ill will towards someone we turn it to love for God, we will avoid all evil. If we deal in hatred, unkindness, lies, or jealousy; it brings nothing but the same.

Knowing that we have the power of The Word and The Word is power and the Word is everything that we say and think; it is the power that is one and the same for good OR bad. Our thoughts, speaks, and actions will reap exactly what we deal in.

This is how I began to change myself, learning this principle, I began a pact with myself that anytime I had an evil or mean thought I would stop it and replace it with good thoughts. Good thoughts about God, thankfulness, and good thoughts about what I can do that is pleasing to God.

This principle became especially helpful during my divorce. I really felt that I was severely wronged. Doesn't everyone that is divorcing? I swear I have never heard a divorcee say "the reason my marriage ended is because I constantly cheated on my wife." The counselor I mentioned earlier also told me that every divorced person leaves as the victim. You never hear a man say "I'm recently divorced; my marriage just fell apart because I was such an asshole." Or a woman say "I was so selfish I spent all of our savings on chronic shopping and refused to have sex with my husband". Isn't that funny! It's so true, even of me; I constantly thought of how he mistreated me and ultimately how he was the reason for our split, our failed businesses and our financial crisis.

I had completely enhanced my faith and felt I had ultimate concern with God, but it was not until I took every evil or negative thought out of my head that I began to receive God's true favor. I am not suggesting to be a push over or smile when someone bad mouths you, but I am saying you will receive twice the reward if you don't deal in hurtful things.

Scripture instructs that when someone talks poorly of us we will actually benefit and be rewarded greatly. There is so much power when we don't deal in negativity. Remember that our mind can conquer all when we only deal in love.

By the divine greatness I was able to understand how to change my life. The difference is this; when we obtain ultimate faith in God, when trouble is around us we possess the power to conquer it. Empowerment from goodness is the most amazing feeling in the entire world.

The power of The Word is the words spoken and thoughts presented through prayer and meditation. The moment we understand that when we do NOT doubt the power we possess is the simultaneous moment true power begins. The activity that we think and speak will come to pass. When peace is established it brings a posture and poise that produces power.

In a sense, God has already done for us all that He can do. He has empowered us with His divine power. Unfortunately, the average person who gains this knowledge will still continue to struggle through life trying to make material of his thoughts through trying to make influential people accept him, trying to influence and impress his boss, or working countless hours to be the best that he can be. The irony is that we possess all of the influence that we will ever need and God already authored our talent, intellect, and attributes for the divine destiny created for us.

If the deep rooted desire we hold in our heart that refuses to die is to be the number one golf champion in the world, no amount of "extra" practice and meeting the right people will bring the dream to reality. Reality will be the moment we become one with Him in faith AND belief. Then it is simply a matter of speaking the word into fruition.

Faith- The obtainment of ultimate concern in God through thinking and speaking with Him and living within His rules.

Belief-The obtainment of one hundred percent knowledge of His promise to provide all of the desires of our heart through the power within us. The level of the conscious thought that is absent of any negative idea OR DOUBT.

BRINGING WORD TO POWER...

John

In the beginning was the Word, and the Word was with God, and the Word was God. The same was in the beginning with God. All things were made by him; and without him was not any thing made that was made.

What is the Word? What do you think the Word means? I absolutely love the way John puts this. It is as if God is speaking directly through John. What John says about the

Word brings immediate peace to me that God intended us to know this important fact. What is the Word? The definition of word is a sound or written form of the sound that symbolizes or communicates a meaning. The Word is everything that comes from your mind. The Word is your thoughts. When God created the world he began with His thoughts…only.

At this point, many Christian biblical experts may say that the word in the beginning is Jesus Christ; and that Jesus was with God in the beginning. It certainly will never be undeniably proven what the actual meaning behind the word is. I believe that the word is the thought which brings the power of creating all through God.

Christians may argue that the word is defined as an uncreated soul that is part of the trinity, therefore proving Jesus to be divine. We must take care when we begin to translate meanings to keep an open mind; understanding that God only furnished us a certain amount of data. If we make the mistake of giving a definitive definition where God intended a mystery there can be a bit of trouble.

Christians believe in a heaven placed somewhere above where our soul spends eternity with God. Many believe in reincarnation. Is it possible that Heaven and Hell are a destiny achieved by the actions of a former life? The most important aspect to remember is that it is a mystery designed to remain just that. Therefore, we must remain open minded to all of the possibilities so as not to judge another's perception. It is sheer arrogance to claim knowledge of the unknown. The one aspect that we KNOW regarding eternal life is His promise of the greatness of it all. Need we know more?

What if Heaven and Hell are here on earth? What if Heaven is the faithful's reincarnated soul coming back as a wealthy and gorgeous country music star? What if Hell is a reincarnated soul immerging back to Earth in poverty or with an addiction for a choice of living unpleasing to God in his former life?

This is farfetched, I realize, but would you make fun of an obese person if you thought that in your next life you would be morbidly obese? Would you frown upon a homosexual if you understood that eternal life for you may mean being born gay in the next life? Would you discriminate against someone not of your race if you knew that in your next life you would be that race?

This is an exaggeration but we must open ourselves to the understanding that God is very clear as to His intention to those who are unkind to others. The promise becomes the wrath. The specifics of Heaven and Hell are a mystery; but the consequences for wrong doing are not. The power of our words can go either way...we must choose them wisely.

But there is no mystery behind the power within us. God is adamant that we are limitless. Can you imagine the possibilities of that?! God said and Jesus reiterated for us that we are the sons and daughters of The Father. We are not simply His creations. We are His children. There is a difference. Scripture says that we are. It may seem insignificant to distinguish the difference, but it is profoundly relevant. If we were simply a living creation of God, we would be much like a tree. God emphasized and Jesus told us we are His children. In Revelations, as well as many other books, it is plainly stated that when we are His children, we will be godlike; we will receive His power because we are part of Him. What an awesome God!

ABUNDANCE AND PROSPERITY

God pleasures in the prosperity of His children...

There is an ongoing controversy that begun long ago regarding God's stance on being wealthy and having earthly possessions. I believe the most commonly quoted bible verse regarding wealth is found in Matthew.

Matthew 19/23-24 when Jesus says:

"Verily I say unto you, that a rich man shall hardly enter into the kingdom of heaven. And again I say unto you, it is easier for a camel to go through the eye of a needle than

> *for a rich man to enter into the kingdom of God."*

This one verse misleads so many to believe that wealthy people cannot walk with faith in God. The story which leads Jesus to this statement is that a young man is requesting advice from Jesus regarding everlasting life. He tells Jesus that he is following God's commandments regarding adultery, stealing, false witness and murder; and now he would like to know if he is" making the cut" in the eyes of God. Jesus instructs the young man to sell all of his possessions and give the proceeds to the poor. It is then reported that the young man walks away sorrowful.

This is a commanding parable, but I think the message is often misunderstood. Whenever reading direct quotes from Jesus, they should be taken very seriously. Jesus wants first and foremost for all of us to understand the requirements for a wonderful life. When you read the entire story, you will notice that all of the commandments are listed *except* the commandments regarding God. The young man lists each commandment he is following; **omitting** the first three(regarding God). This is **key**. Jesus did not say that wealthy people cannot enter heaven; He said it is difficult. He knew it is difficult because *most* wealthy people have put money in front of love for God.

He also knew that once people obtain wealth, they historically forget about God or begin to love other things that are now at their disposal. Here lies the difficulty; but not the impossibility. *This is so important*; it is easy to love God climbing to prosperity. Praying every day as your life begins to change and you are seeing His favor is easy. However, once you get there, it is essential to be humble, charitable, and **stay** in faith. Remember to give thanks every day, all day! Highlight in your bible, this book, your other spiritual books, and read them every day to remind you to stay in faith.

In this particular story, it is my guess that the young man was a good person, doing all of the right things in reference to himself and his neighbors; but he was putting money at the top of his priorities. God was second; not way down on the list, but second on his list. Jesus told this particular individual to sell all of his possessions because He felt it the only way for this young man to learn the error of his ways. It is only when we completely let go of what is first on our priority list that God can take first priority; it's a common sense lesson Jesus wanted us to understand out of His love for us.

The next verse after the camel and needle confirms Jesus' intention in His message. The apostles basically question the advice he gives the young man by asking, "so rich people won't go to heaven?" And His answer is this; with God, all things are possible.

He *never* said it is impossible. What He said is that it is *only* possible when you are in faith with God.

There are far too many times in both testaments that God promises wealth. He doesn't promise ample; He promises abundance. It is a dishonor to our God to short change ourselves of the luxuries of life. I am positive that God loves to see His children succeed and reap the rewards that

He has in store for them. But the danger lies in forgetting what is important. The best verse to me that gives the epitome of God's expectations of us regarding wealth is in Deuteronomy.

Deuteronomy 8/13-15,17

And when thy herds and thy flocks multiply, and thy silver and thy gold is multiplied; Then thine heart be lifted up, and thou forget the LORD thy God, which brought thee forth out of the land of Egypt, from the house of bondage; Who led thee through that great and terrible wilderness

And thou say in thine heart, my power and the might of mine hand hath gotten me this wealth.

How powerful the precision of those words! I feel peace knowing now in my adult life that my God encourages me to have the desires of my heart. He only discourages putting wealth before Him *and* forgetting Him once we receive. Just as our earthly parents are fearful of their children acquiring wealth before they are responsible enough to do the right things, so feels our Father. He wants us to enjoy ourselves and not get into trouble. Also, if your parents were nothing but loving and kind to you, and you were nothing but the same to them; how would they feel if they gave you your inheritance early, and you never called them again?

Many people, I am sure, have made the mistake of following God in faith, and then abandoning Him when they receive His favor. Fortunately for us, God is kind enough to give us the consequence for this action, He says we will perish. In my opinion, a person will not technically perish. I believe that without seeing the error in forgetting faith, a person will lose favor. For example, if an actress that lives with faith in God finally lands the role of a life time and receives that great salary she has been praying for only to never pray again, I think she will eventually lose the role as well as the salary. It's not karma, it's not fate, it's the power we receive in faith. It can go either way.

I also love in verse 17 God further warns that if a person is vane enough to think that the bestselling book she wrote or the invention she patented or even the man she married is the *source* of her income, she will not have favor in God's eyes. It is so important to understand that the source of everything we possess is from God; and God only. The moment a person starts to think that it is his own intellect or ideas that has brought wealth to him, is the moment it can be taken away.

When you have faith in God, and it is wealth you want; wealth you will have. The Bible expresses God's promise of this in too many verses to count. Jesus also boldly tells us to ask and we shall receive. There is nothing whatsoever wrong with asking God for money or wealth. Be ready to receive it; just never forget Who blessed you and always stay in faith.

CHAPTER 11} THE RAINMAKER

The cities in scripture, although a geographic location, are also representative of people and their current state. Israel is symbolic of our job, our happiness, our well-being, our wealth, and our health.

When Jacob receives favor, God actually changes his name to Israel.

It is beautifully symbolic of a new beginning. Jacob will now receive the power of God. What better way to show that everything is different now than the changing of a name? I believe that God is telling Jacob "You did it and I am so proud of you. Welcome to My kingdom, are you ready to receive all that I have promised you?"

I love rain. I'm from one of the rainiest cities in the states; Mobile, Alabama. But in St. Louis, it is hit or miss for needed rain. Often, summers in St. Louis can be very hot. Homeowners strive throughout the season to keep their grass green by watering in the early morning until the grass is satisfactorily saturated. It is easy to observe the ones faithful to the health of their grass. But what is striking is that no amount of fertilizer and water can achieve the startling greenness observed after a rain from God. I love to marvel at the grass and leaves on the trees after heaven rains. The bright crisp hue can only be described as brilliant with a hint of vibrant blue and striking pure golden yellow for the most outstanding green imaginable. I gaze out the window again and again to witness it.

It is a parable for life. We can try with every fiber of energy, hard work, and high goals (like sprinklers and fertilizer) to achieve the best life imaginable but it will pale in comparison to the life that God can provide. Just like a rain from God, the result requires no physical involvement on our part, only the wisdom in the belief that it can be provided by no other source. When we attempt to accomplish our prayer through the materials of man we will only receive the result that man can provide. When we receive His favor, however, the result will be like the surreal color of green after a God given rain; spectacular!

"The Lord shall open unto thee His good treasure, the heaven to give the rain unto thy land in his season, and to bless all of the work of thine hand: and thou shalt lend unto many nations, and thou shalt not borrow."

God said in Deuteronomy Chapter 28; those who follow will be lenders and not borrowers, they will be the head and not the tail, they will always be above and not below and rain will bless their crops.

Rain is happiness, health, and prosperity now as it was thousands of years ago. It enables us absolutely everything we need to prosper and live in abundance and bliss. It takes extreme effort to survive the desert but the rain forest is filled with greenness from Heaven above.

We are Rainmakers. Through our words, thoughts, and actions we can make it rain. The key is through the scripture and the spoken word, we hold the power of a Rainmaker. Speak out scripture daily with your own words. Find every word written that brings you peace and speak it into fruition.

Live in faith first then...

If it's a baby you are believing for; speak every word you know of God mixed with your own...

Father, you said that the faithful shall not be barren, I love you and believe that you will bless me with children.

Father, after Rachel was barren, you blessed her womb and gave her two sons. Father, I believe in you and I will live in your ways, I believe that I will be blessed like Rachel.

If you are lonely and haven't met the right person...

Father, just as Ruth was given Boaz, I believe because I now live in faith with you I will meet the person of my dreams.

Father, you said I would have the desires of my heart and I know that I will meet the right person soon.

If you are ill, live in faith and belief telling God...

Father, you promised the faithful would live many years, I know I will be healed. I thank you the answer is on the way.

It is my sincere desire that those reading this book will transform into the son or daughter he or she was created and destined to be. I believe that seeking to have a perfect relationship with God is the secret to a victorious and happy life. If we are seeking Him, we are living pleasing onto Him.

There is nothing He would like to see more than us enjoying our kids, our life, our vacation, our beautiful new home, our awesome new wardrobe with the best body we can have.

I believe that God is beaming when he sees us take that money and help another family, pay someone's rent, give a couple in the grocery store an extra twenty or an extra hundred if we have it. Pay to get someone out of a third world country or pay for their tuition at a great university. God uses His children to help His other children. "Surely goodness and mercy shall follow me, all the days of my life: and I will dwell in the house of the Lord forever."

God is the same now as He was yesterday and forever will be. Some religious groups believe that because God is always the same and never changes, that our paths or destiny has an intricate timeline with an ending result with every occurrence planned and set with no possibility of another result. In other words, every aspect of our life has been predetermined from whom we marry to how many children we will have to our precise method and time of death.

Based on my studies, I disagree. I believe that each individual has been administered a certain degree of faith. The Bible prerequisites what a person receives based on the way he lives life that each individual has many scenarios based on free will; man's decision to live in faith or live in absence of it.

You can lead a horse to water, but you cannot make him drink. Free will is the greatest tool to lead us to faith and the greatest deterrent to keep us from it.

The map to success is hidden within the testaments old and new with clarity and obvious intention. Those of us who believe in the Power and live accordingly through His statutes will receive the Power of eternal life, victory, abundant prosperity, happiness, wholeness, richness, unsurpassable health and the ultimate life of all goodness.

Jesus was a human on Earth and died for our sins. It is the greatest gift we could receive. But second to what he gave us in death, with relevance to our salvation, is the gift He gave us in example of how to live. The popular phrase that was coined "what would Jesus do?" has merit far beyond the marketable intention of the words.

Jesus showed us every living example of how to live, what to strive for, what rules are important to God, what is received based on the transformation, and most importantly, how God reigns. The how and the why of what God controls is astronomical in terms of faith because of His omnipotence.

How many of us are turned away from faith because of the death or misfortune of a loved one? How many of us doubt his ultimate concern for us based on the current state of events or a specific outcome?

If God miraculously cured my aunt from pancreatic cancer and the physician reading the latest results of her oncology results labeled it a miracle, then God is ultimately to blame for my brother who died instantly from a motorcycle accident.

But when we look to the story of John the Baptist, we can clearly ascertain that death of a loved one even happened to Jesus. John was beheaded for the most senseless motive a person can imagine; his head was wanted as a gift. If John the Baptist, who was depicted as inherently a great man who lived his life to spread the will of God was brutally murdered, isn't that definitive proof that death is not a place by which God *always* intervenes? God should have intervened for His own son, right? But the truth is that we may never know why a young child suffers or why an entire family is killed in a car accident during the Christmas holidays. But to live a life absent of faith due to the mystery of death is a tragedy greater than death; because it is a lifeless life.

Jesus taught us differently. Jesus was so human; he was kind, giving, loving, and caring. But he was also confused, angry, sarcastic, and tempted at times as well. He had friends that betrayed him, used him, and talked about him behind His back. His cousin was brutally slain. He had strangers that plotted against Him and He was constantly questioned as to His authenticity as well as His motives. He got irritated when His friends needed further demonstration and didn't hesitate to call them out on it (oh ye of little faith).

He showed us that every person is God's child. His friends were some of the biggest sinners and He loved them unconditionally. His family was commoners. Even they doubted His divine power. But He lived for His Father and never considered approval of man; only working for the approval of The Father. In return, He received the Power and insisted upon the fact that all of mankind has the same entitlement and inheritance. ***Jesus said everyone that believes will unlock the power that He himself possesses.***

He was the finest living example of how we should treat the people who set out religiously to destroy us. He willingly received immeasurable excruciating pain for every soul.

He received eternal life and blessing with The Father. Whether you personally believe in His divinity or not; His life on Earth was the complete example and blueprint to becoming all that God wants of us.

And when we look to the words of The Old Testament…

Deuteronomy 30:19-20

I call Heaven and Earth to record this day against you, that I have set before you life and death, blessing and cursing: therefore choose life, that both thou and thy seed may live:

That thou mayest love the Lord thy God, and that thou mayest obey his voice, and that thou mayest cleave unto him: for he is thy life, and the length of thy days: that thou mayest live in the land that which the Lord sware unto thy fathers…

Eternal heaven both here on Earth and after lies within the pages of scripture. We can live our entire life being a good person; but until we take a hold of the reins and learn and live with faith in God, we will not live in the ultimate bliss He intended.

Take your treasure now. Make it rain.

The End

151 | P a g e

Dear Reader;

I cannot thank you enough for purchasing my book. It is my sincere hope that it becomes a tool you utilize to thrust you into all that God has planned for you. My promise to you is that you can do this; you can fulfill your divine destiny and it is grand!

If you were inspired by this book, please take a moment to write a review at the site in which you purchased it. Often when we are deciding if a book is right for us, words from others can be the determining factor. Your story or what this book did for you could be the nudge someone needed to begin the journey.

Look for my next release, The Clandestine Order, in May 2014. It is an inspirational book about the people in today's modern society who possess the Great Power.

Again, my sincere appreciation for reading my work. May you live a blissfully successful and happy life walking in faith with God.

My deepest love,

-Karen

153 | P a g e

CPSIA information can be obtained
at www.ICGtesting.com
Printed in the USA
LVHW081135300619
622770LV00023B/1549/P